Stock Index Options and Futures

Stock Index Options and Futures

JOHN MILLERS

McGRAW-HILL BOOK COMPANY

London · New York · St Louis · San Francisco · Auckland
Bogotá · Caracas · Hamburg · Lisbon · Madrid · Mexico
Milan · Montreal · New Delhi · Panama · Paris · San Juan
São Paulo · Singapore · Sydney · Tokyo · Toronto

Published by
McGRAW-HILL Book Company Europe
Shoppenhangers Road, Maidenhead, Berkshire, SL6 2QL, England
Telephone 0628 23432
Fax 0628 770224

British Library Cataloguing in Publication Data

Millers, John
  Stock Index Options and Futures
  I. Title
  332.64

  ISBN 0-07-707686-9

Library of Congress Cataloging-in-Publication Data

Millers, John,
    Stock index options and futures / John Millers.
      p.   cm.
    Includes bibliographical references and index.
    ISBN 0-07-707686-9 (H/B)
    1. Stock index futures.   2. Options (Finance)   3. Stock index
  futures—Europe.   I. Title.
  HG6043.M55   1992   92-14697
  332.63'228—dc20   CIP

1234   CUP   9432

Typeset by Cambridge Composing (UK) Ltd
and printed and bound at the University Press, Cambridge

Contents

Acknowledgements

The author wishes to thank all the many friends and colleagues who either wittingly or unwittingly assisted in the production of this book. Just a few years ago, when the author first embarked on his career, stock index products as such did not exist. Today they are widespread, and their development still continues. This 'newness' of both concept and development, as well as the very wide number of other disciplines upon which stock indices impinge, has meant that the author has drawn inspiration from a very large number of different people. To all of them I express my sincerest thanks.

In particular, I should like to thank my good friend and colleague, Malcolm Robertson, for his not insignificant role in 'getting me into this in the first place', as well as the considerable technical help subsequently!

My thanks also to Alan Johnson of Market Directional Analysis for his many useful thoughts on technical analysis; Deborah Owen, editor of *The Speculator*, for permission to reuse my example on option pricing (page 72) which was originally published in *The Speculator* in October 1989; and the considerable assistance from the London International Financial Futures Exchange in providing background information.

John Millers

CHAPTER 1

Past and present

Life is risk. Consciously or unconsciously we may seek to make our lives more secure, but an element of risk is always present. Often, to gain a higher level of security, we have to undergo a period of increased risk. It is little wonder then that futures contracts, which were developed specifically for the elimination of price risk, are seen by many as highly speculative financial instruments more suited to those who frequent race courses and casinos, rather than those charged with the responsibility of managing money, either their own or, more particularly, that of others.

While many countries have at times banned futures and options trading, not really being convinced of their commercial benefits, stock index contracts in particular had an even more difficult start. In order to control gambling, many governments around the world constructed well-meaning anti-gambling laws—gambling or gaming itself often being defined as the 'payment of money on the outcome of an event'. Unfortunately this definition immediately sweeps the possibility of trading on an index into the gambling camp, as underlying the contract is not a physical product or even a government bond, but just numbers, and the participants are clearly 'betting' on the future level of the stock market.

These views have now changed—stock index derivatives have gained respectability and are currently being traded in almost every part of the world where there is a stock exchange.

The origins of formal futures contracts

Before starting to investigate index derivatives, it is as well to remind ourselves why futures contracts developed—in order to eliminate price risk. Although various examples of the forward pricing of many products can be traced back through to medieval times, 'forward pricing' was only 'regularized' for a few specific commodities by the Chicago Board of Trade in 1848. Formal futures trading was subsequently established in 1865, at the time of the American Civil War and at a time when the prices of staple commodities such as grain and cotton would fluctuate dramatically and often quite unpredictably. The result of all this wild price movement was that the producers, mainly the farmers, had no idea from one day to the next just what they could expect for their goods. The buyers and processors on the other hand had no control over their expenditures. All parties could see the benefits of having a contractural form where forward prices could be fixed. Thus the mechanism of futures contracts was created and formalized specifically for the purpose of eliminating price risk. If a producer found that the price currently available on the futures market was attractive, he could sell his goods 'forward', and know that when he came to deliver, the predetermined price was the one he would receive, no matter what had happened to the market in the interim.

From such agricultural beginnings, many different 'physical' futures contracts have developed: coffee, soyabean meal, fresh orange juice, sugar, greasy wool as well as many contracts for industrial and precious metals.

A totally new field of activity was opened up with the introduction, in 1972, of an entirely new variety of contract. The International Monetary Market (IMM, a division of the Chicago Mercantile Exchange) started trading currency futures. Financial futures were born. Within a short space of time the Chicago Board of Trade (CBOT) introduced the GNMA, a Government National Mortgage Association contract. In 1976 the IMM launched its Treasury Bill future, and in 1977 the CBOT started trading the Treasury Bond future. This latter contract has since become one of the most actively traded futures contracts in the world, and gave considerable impetus to other futures exchanges around the world to develop interest rate futures contracts. Today, interest rate futures contracts attract the greatest trading volume of any futures contracts; where new futures exchanges are opened, the first contract to be introduced is inevitably one based on a domestic bond, bill, gilt or bund. As a result, these financial futures instruments have become an accepted instrument of controlling investment or monitoring interest rate risks.

Stock index contract development

Stock index contracts, when they finally came, were in a way just as revolutionary an idea compared to interest rate or currency contracts as they themselves had been when looked at from the traditional stable of physical commodities. For the first time a contract was created based not on a readily deliverable physical commodity or currency or negotiable deposit instrument, but on a concept—the concept of a mathematically measurable index based on the market movement of a predetermined number of equities.

While the idea of trading an index was a new concept, it was easy to see the economic advantage that such a product could provide. All investors whether individual or institutional are exposed to market risks; a stock index futures contract could be used to hedge such risks during periods of market decline, or simply allow the investor to take a view on the direction of the whole market without the need for selecting a portfolio of stocks. The idea of using an index for judging market movement was in any case already in place—the Dow Jones Industrial Average was well known and respected. It seemed on the face of it easy enough to multiply up the Dow by a certain number of dollars a point to give a futures contract.

Such elegant ideas, sadly, rarely come to fruition. It might have been expected that stock index futures would first have been developed either on the established futures exchanges in Chicago, or close to the centre of the American Stock Exchange in New York. How galling it must have been for these two markets to see the lead stolen from them by the Kansas City Board of Trade (KCBT), a regional wheat market that was looking for ways to break into new markets and capitalize on the growth that they had seen as a result of the huge increase in wheat sales to the Soviet Union during the 1970s. Planners at the KCBT applied to the Commodity Futures Trading Commission (CFTC), the federal agency responsible for the futures industry, to trade a futures contract based on '30 industrial stocks'. At the same time a request was made to Dow Jones & Co. to allow the KCBT to use its 'Industrial Average' for futures trading. Dow Jones was horrified.

The thought that its index might be used as the basis for gambling by a pack of futures brokers, caused severe apoplexy at senior levels. It told the KCBT to forget any thoughts it might have had for such a contract, and indeed if the matter was pursued, Dow Jones & Co would sue for damaging its name by associating it with such a venture!

The KCBT did not feel like pursuing this through the courts, so instead turned to Standard & Poor's (S & P)—another good idea, but S & P was already talking to the Chicago Mercantile Exchange. It was the Value Line Index of Arnold Bernhard & Company that the KCBT was finally able to secure as the underlying instrument of their futures contract. Contrary to the two previous attempts, Arnold Bernhard was actually quite keen to let the Value Line be so used. The KCBT amended its application to the CFTC to use the Value Line as the underlying index on its futures contract, and then started to wait for approval. . . .

Meanwhile, as the Chicago Mercantile Exchange (CME) was cementing its relationship with Standard and Poor's, it obtained exclusive rights to use the S & P as the underlying index for its futures contract while the New York Futures Exchange (NYFE) naturally looked to develop a contract based on the composite index of its parent, the New York Stock Exchange (NYSE). This all left the CBOT feeling that it might miss out on a potentially lucrative market, and as the choice of possible indices was now dwindling, the CBOT decided to persuade, either with money or through the courts, Dow Jones & Co to allow its Industrial Average to be used. Dow Jones & Co was still horrified. It maintained that having its name linked with what was then perceived to be a purely speculative trading instrument would bring it into disrepute. Unless the CBOT dropped the idea, Dow Jones & Co would go to court to prevent the move. The CBOT was in a fighting mood; soon lawsuits and countersuits had been filed in the state and federal courts in Chicago, New York and even Washington. Stock index contracts were certainly good news for the legal profession, particularly as the S & P also filed a copyright infringement suit against Comex, the New York Commodities Exchange, because they were attempting to launch a futures contract based on the 'Comex 500' stocks. These had a curious likeness to the stocks listed under S & P 500.

The courts found in favour of both S & P, and Dow Jones. Comex and the CBOT withdrew to consider alternative indices, but the publicity had created considerable debate. Arguments for and against index or 'portfolio' futures raged and contributed to the general confusion at the CFTC, which was also now asked to give evidence before several Congressional committees seeking to determine whether these 'portfolio' futures might not be against the public interest. Constantly, the main argument against these index contracts was that as there was nothing at the end of the contract, other than the transfer of monies based on who was up and who was down when the contract expired, it was clearly only another way to gamble. Additionally, if this new 'game' was legalized and became significant, could not these futures contracts at some time have a detrimental effect on the underlying equity markets. . . . ?

Finally, in early 1982 the CFTC approved the introduction of stock index contracts, and as the KCBT application had been the first submitted, it was the first to be approved, four and a half years after the original application. Instantly, the KCBT attempted to block the approval of the other applications on the grounds that the KCBT needed to recoup its investment before opening the market to completion, but this was rejected. Trading started in the Kansas City Value Line Index Future (KCVLIF) on 24 February 1982. This was almost immediately followed by the launch of the S & P 500 index future on the CME in April, and in May the NYFE started trading in the NYSE composite index future.

The CBOT, which now seemed to be left on the sidelines, entered into discussions with the KCBT suggesting that the two exchanges might trade the Value Line jointly. The KCBT was not terribly interested. Finally, the CBOT reached an agreement with the American Stock Exchange to trade a contract, to be known as the Major Market Index (MMI), based on 20 blue-chip stocks in its listing. At long last, in August of 1983, the CBOT also had its own stock index contract, in a market that was by now showing spectacular growth, and developing options contracts on the futures.

Definitions and other considerations

A *stock index futures contract* is a legally binding contract that fixes
the level at which the underlying index can be purchased or sold
at a specific future date. A *stock index option* is the right to buy or
sell a fixed quantity of the underlying index at a fixed level at or
before a specific date in the future.

While in a futures contract both parties are legally committed
once the position is opened, in an options contract the seller of the
option, call or put, is legally bound to perform at the buyer's
'option'.

The home of formal stock index contracts is regarded as America, although it is interesting to note that in Europe several earlier
attempts were made to develop index trading. Most of these
attempts were outside the official exchanges, but from time to time
it has been possible to trade forward contracts on the Dow Jones
Industrial Average and the Financial Times 30 Share Index in
several European countries, particularly in Amsterdam during the
1970s.

The supposedly novel way of using an index as the basis for a
futures contract in fact is not unique. It can be argued that
Treasury Bond or Gilt futures, for instance, in fact represent a
comprehensive view of a wide range of long-term debt instruments.
Eurodollar futures are explicitly based on an index. Consequently,
all the arguments decrying stock index contracts as just a form of
gambling because settlement can only be in cash, therefore, do not
really stand up. Even in physical commodity contracts, settlement
is in cash for most of the time as over 80 per cent of commodity
contracts are not taken to expiry. In financial contracts this
proportion can be even higher. The futures markets are used in
order to hedge a financial risk, as well as to take a speculative view
or strategic investment decision; for most of the time the physical
items themselves are handled away from the futures exchanges.

Cash settlement of contracts actually has several benefits. Convergence of the futures price with the spot or cash price is
guaranteed because the final settlement price is imposed on the
market. The uncertainties of physical delivery are eliminated—
there are no quality worries, no problems associated in receiving
the 'cheapest to deliver' (i.e. poorest acceptable quality), which
can also translate into concerns about squeezes on near contracts,

corners or sheer inability to deliver because of warehouse conges-
tion. Investors, traders and hedgers can maintain their positions in
the maturing contract right through to settlement without any
worries about market liquidity or orderly settlement. A significant
percentage of stock index contract open positions (those positions
held open, if not matched off) will be run to expiry in any case, as
many contracts will have been opened either as arbitrage trades
requiring compensating trades in the equity market at the moment
of futures expiry, or as hedge positions for dealers making a market
in stock index options contracts. For this reason options contracts
that are compatible with futures will require to expire concurrently.

The dramatic growth of stock index contracts

Undoubtedly stock index contracts have been one of the great
successes of the 1980s. In America the S & P 500 future and S & P
100 options contracts have been particularly successful. The S & P
500 future, which on its first day of trading achieved 3963 contracts,
had within five years become the world's second largest futures
contract in the world (exceeded only by the Treasury Bond), and
with a volume in the months leading up to the crash of October
1987 of 80 000 contracts per day. On many days over 100 000
contracts were achieved. In money terms, with the S & P 500 at
320.00 and the contract valued at US$ 500 a point, the underlying
value traded represents about (US$ 500 × 320 × 80 000) =
US$ 12 800 million of equivalent equity value, far more than the
actual value of equities traded on the New York Stock Exchange.

Figure 1.1 shows us the growth in both trading volume and open
interest since the introduction of the S & P 500 futures contract.
The general pattern confirms that as well as attracting very healthy
short-term trading volumes, the contract has also been increasingly
used as a long-term strategic investment tool, and in this respect
was not affected by the crash in October 1987. After the crash,
volumes of trading, as opposed to the open interest, were reduced
by about 40 per cent for 1988 and much of 1989. Accusations that
dealing in stock index contracts had made the crash far worse than
it might have been otherwise have never been proven. Many
accusations seemed to originate from various lobbies looking for a
scapegoat for their equity losses. This did result in the introduction
of an elaborate system of so-called 'circuit breakers' that limit daily

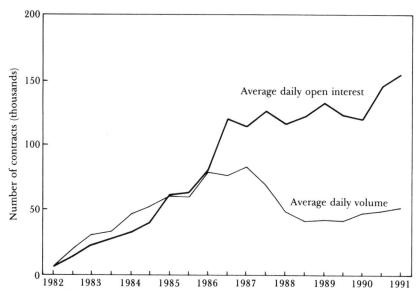

Figure 1.1   S & P 500 futures contracts (figures based on six-monthly averages)

price moves to a limited number of points below the previous day's settlement price, as well as holding up futures trading until at least 50 per cent of the underlying stocks are also trading.

Restrictions such as these do dampen down excessive volatility, and have been introduced in various markets from time to time. Some purists argue that the introduction of any constraints inhibits a free market. On the other hand, the knowledge that constraints exist can sometimes be enough of a market force to preserve a more 'orderly' market without having to trigger limit thresholds.

Volumes on the S & P 500 have been returning but currently pride of place for numbers of contracts traded by an index contract is now taken by the S & P 100 option. In 1990 this traded a massive total of nearly 69 000 000 contracts, far more than any other index contract in the world. The S & P 500 future is still one of the major contracts, but is now in second place to the Nikkei 225 future traded in Osaka, a reflection of the growing importance of the Japanese market.

Even before the American markets launched their stock index contracts, stock and futures exchanges around the world were already considering how they might develop their own index derivative contracts once the American ones had been shown to be successful.

The Sydney Futures Exchange was fairly quick off the mark, introducing a futures contract on the Australian Stock Exchange All Ordinaries Index in February 1983. This index, based on 250 of the most commonly traded shares on the Sydney and Melbourne stock markets, account for about 90 per cent of the value of all shares listed on the Australian stock market. The Australian index contract proved very successful and increased volumes sharply with the introduction of an option on the future in 1984. By 1986 combined futures and options were achieving in excess of 100 000 contracts per day.

Within a year of the launch of the Australian stock index future, futures or index options contracts were rapidly being introduced in many of the world's major exchanges. The UK started trading the FT-SE 100 Index on the London International Financial Futures Exchange (LIFFE) in February 1984. An important missing major market, the Japanese, was finally represented in September 1986 when SIMEX, the Singapore-based exchange introduced a contract on the Nikkei Stock Average. At the time the Japanese themselves were still struggling with legislation to enable them to trade a 'non-deliverable' product.

Today, particularly with the development of the domestic derivatives markets in Japan, volumes of index futures and options contracts traded on a worldwide basis have mushroomed. Volume figures for the top 20 traded contracts are given in Table 1.1. It gives the total volume figures for 1990 and is revealing on several points. It is no great surprise to see the top six places divided between American and Japanese contracts, and for their traded volumes to be comparable to and generally greater than the actual underlying equity volumes traded in these markets. Much more of a surprise is to see the index option on the Swedish market taking seventh place, and the Swiss represented at number eight. Interestingly, the two French index contracts, with their much shorter history than the UK FT-SE contracts are already overtaking the volumes of the UK market with its much larger equity base. In this respect, the ranking of contracts tells us something about 'national investment characteristics', and the legislation that goes with them.

The UK may have suffered to a degree from confused legislation

Table 1.1   Major stock index contracts for 1990

Position	Contract		Exchange	Volume 1990
1	S & P 100	O	CBOE	68 800 000
2	Nikkei 225	F	Osaka	13 600 000
3	S & P 500	F	CME	12 100 000
4	S & P 500	O	CBOE	12 100 000
5	Nikkei 225	O	Osaka	9 200 000
6	MMI	O	Amex	5 600 000
7	OMX	O	SwOM	5 200 000
8	SMI	O	Soffex	4 700 000
9	TOPIX	F	TSE	2 800 000
10	FT-SE 100	O	LTOM	2 400 000
11	CAC-40	O	Monep	2 400 000
12	IBOVESPA	F	BM & F	2 300 000
13	Dutch SI	O	EOE	1 700 000
14	S & P 500	O	CME	1 600 000
15	CAC	F	MATIF	1 600 000
16	NYSE Comp	F	NYFE	1 600 000
17	FT-SE 100	F	LIFFE	1 400 000
18	MMI	F	CBOT	1 000 000
19	Nikkei Dow	F	SIMEX	900 000
20	All Ord	F	SFE	300 000

Source: 'Futures and Options World', London, February 1991, Metal Bulletin plc.

(in the past), but that cannot be the reason why trading volumes are not higher. The graph in Figure 1.2, a UK equivalent of the S & P graph in Figure 1.1, shows trading volumes and open interest on the FT-SE 100 Index future since trading started.

Figure 1.2 shows that while the open interest has shown impressive growth, representing long-term strategic investment use of the market by major institutions, trading volumes have grown much more slowly and are at present only about one-fifth of the open interest. By comparison, the S & P 500 graph (Figure 1.1) shows a much closer correlation between daily trading volumes and open interest, and is more typical of index futures contracts generally, where the daily trading volumes oscillate between 50 and 80 per cent of the open interest. One can only infer that the average UK investor has not yet developed as much of a trading attitude to investment as have many of his overseas competitors.

A list of all index contracts currently traded is included in Appendix 2, although many more contracts are currently at the

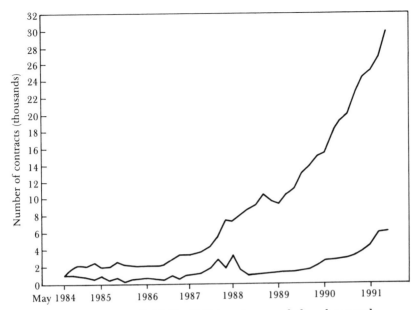

Figure 1.2 LIFFE FT-SE 100 Future (average daily volume and
month-end open interest)

planning stage and could be introduced soon. At the last count the
USA alone had 22 index futures and options contracts that
currently trade; over the last few years at least five new index
contracts have been introduced and withdrawn. The rest of the
world so far has over 45 contracts currently trading. It may not be
very long before we see an index contract on one of the new stock
exchanges developing in the once communist economies of eastern
Europe. A Warsaw or Budapest stock index is probably only a
matter of time—a stock index traded on a Moscow exchange still
seems some way off, but in the post-communist era it now seems
an inevitability that was once unbelievable.

As indexation progresses around the world, it becomes easier to
create an index of leading companies from around the globe, use
them to judge how equity markets may be performing on a global
basis and, hence, see how one part of the world is performing
against the rest. It is already possible to trade a European index,
and in due course it will be possible to trade a global index. The
opportunities raised by such instruments are discussed in the final
chapter.

CHAPTER 2

Index construction

The Dow Jones and arithmetic means

In order to quantify how the American stock market was performing, the two editors of the 'Customers Afternoon Letter' started in
1884 to publish irregularly the average closing price of 11 'active
and representative' stocks. This number, which indicated market
movement, was the first attempt by Charles H. Dow and Edward
D. Jones to provide a stock index.

Dow's early calculations were based on nine railroad stocks and
two industrials. At the time railroad stocks were regarded as a
good, solid investment; all else tended to be viewed as wildly
speculative! At the end of the day Dow simply added up the closing
prices of the 11 stocks and divided the total by 11. This gave what
is commonly known as an *arithmetic mean*, and is the usual form of
calculation made whenever we want to know the average or mean
of a list of numbers. To give a simple example, the arithmetic
mean of five stocks, priced respectively at 10, 12, 14, 16, 18 is:

$$\frac{10 + 12 + 14 + 16 + 18}{5} = 14$$

Over the next few years, following Dow's publication of the original
list of 11 stocks, manufacturing enterprises which had been small
and isolated started to amalgamate into larger industrial complexes.
American Tobacco, General Electric and US Rubber followed the
earlier example of the tie-up that created The Standard Oil Trust in
1879. These merged industrial corporations started to overtake the
railroads in capitalization, financial requirements increased propor-

Table 2.1 The Dow Jones Industrial Average 30 stocks (March 1991)

Allied-Sig	International Paper
Alcoa	McDonalds
American Express	Merck
American T & T	Minnesota Mining & Mfg
Bethlehem Steel	Navistar
Boeing	Philip Morris
Chevron	Primerica
Coca Cola	Procter & Gamble
Du Pont	Sears, Roebuck
Eastman Kodak	Texaco
Exxon	USX
General Electric	Union Carbine
General Motors	United Technologies
Goodyear	Westinghouse
IBM	Woolworth

tionately, and the volume of shares issued and traded in these now more respectable industrials increased dramatically.

Dow's list started to change and, within 10 years of the original index, the new list consisted almost entirely of industrial stocks, becoming known as the Dow Jones Industrial Average that we know today.

Although Dow died in 1902, the index continued to be improved, modified and expanded until by 1928 it had reached 30 stocks, the same number as used today (Table 2.1). It is a sobering thought that only one of the original 30 stocks is still recognizable in the Dow Jones today, namely General Electric, and less than half of the remainder can be traced back to an existence in 1928. Blue-chip stocks of today need not be those of tomorrow—a delightful consideration that throws under scrutiny the very concept of blue-chippedness.

One of the immediate problems that we have with a simple arithmetic mean based index is that of share splits. If the $10 stock on our previous example has a two for one split, the new price would be half the old one so our average would be:

$$\frac{5 + 12 + 14 + 16 + 18}{5} = 13$$

We now have an apparent decline of the index, while holders of the equities would not actually be any worse off financially. Dow's initial solution to this problem was to count the new $5 stock twice, but as such splits became more frequent and repeated on particular stocks, calculation of a simple arithmetic mean became complex, and a new technique of calculation was sought.

The solution that Dow Jones & Co adopted (in 1928) was to change the division every time there was a share split.

$$\frac{5 + 12 + 14 + 16 + 18}{4.643} = 14$$

This restores our average back to the original number, but the divisor is no longer representative of the number of stocks in the index.

Although the list of 30 leading industrial companies that make up the Dow do give a very good representation of what the American blue-chip market is doing, it does have a significant limitation. There is no allowance for the size of the company. Clearly it should be more important that a stock with a very large capitalization rises 1 cent than a 1 cent rise on a very small company. Notwithstanding this limitation, the Dow Jones is still regarded as the major indicator of the health of the American stock market.

The Standard & Poor's 500 Index and capitalization weighting

Although Henry Varnum Poor began publication of corporate and investment information some 20 years before Dow & Jones started their activities, it was only in 1946 that the Standard & Poor's Corporation began publication of their 500 Index. Because of the number of stocks used it is very much more representative of the 'US stock market' and has therefore become a yardstick against which other US stocks as well as funds are judged.

The 500 stocks used to compile the index come from four main categories: 400 industrials, 40 public utilities, 20 transportations and 40 financial institutions. Today, the companies are selected not just on capitalization, but on the basis that they are represent- ative of a particular industry and that their share movements are sensitive to changes in that industry. The four main categories of the S & P 500 are broken down further into some 90 industrial groupings, and the inherent dynamism of the S & P 500 ensures that not only can individual shares be dropped from or added to the index, but whole new industrial sectors are occasionally created pushing out others that are no longer viable in their own right.

The S & P 500 is a capitalization-weighted index. Each stock price change therefore affects the index in direct proportion to its capitalization. A large corporation rising 10 cents will have a much more significant effect on the index than a very small company rising 10 cents. To calculate the index, firstly, each stock must be 'weighted'. This is done by multiplying the price of the share by the number of shares in the market. Once this is done for all 500 shares in the index, we obtain the total capitalization of the index. This capitalization figure is then expressed as a percentage of the average market value of the 500 stocks during the defined base period, 1941 to 1943. Finally, this percentage is divided by 10 to produce the actual number that we see when we look at the S & P 500. As the multiplication of share prices by the number of shares outstanding automatically adjusts for any stock splits, there is no need for any adjustment or rebalancing of the divisor, as in the Dow Jones.

Example of the calculation of a capitalization-weighted index

If we assume that our simple index is to be made up of just four shares, A, B, C and D, with market prices and numbers of issued shares as shown, we can calculate individual and total market capitalization as follows:

Share	Price	Total no of shares	Capitalization
A	20	4 000	80 000
B	60	5 000	300 000
C	145	2 000	290 000
D	15	10 000	150 000
			820 000

Our market, therefore, has a total capitalization value of 820 000 price units. We can now calculate our index allowing for the different weightings as follows:

$$\text{index} = \left(\frac{20 \times 4000}{820\ 000}\right) + \left(\frac{60 \times 5000}{820\ 000}\right) + \left(\frac{145 \times 2000}{820\ 000}\right) + \left(\frac{15 \times 10\ 000}{820\ 000}\right)$$

$$\text{index} = \quad 0.098 \quad + \quad 0.366 \quad + \quad 0.354 \quad + \quad 0.183$$

$$= \quad 1.00$$

This answer should not be a surprise—we are after all just adding up fractions of a whole. Should we now wish our original index to start at a number of 1000, we simply multiply the index by 1000. If we assume that the market now rises evenly by 20 per cent, we would expect our index also to rise by 20 per cent. Reworking the calculation using share prices that have increased by 20 per cent, but using the original total capitalization, we get:

$$\text{new index} = \left(\frac{24 \times 4000}{820\ 000}\right) + \left(\frac{72 \times 5000}{820\ 000}\right) + \left(\frac{174 \times 2000}{820\ 000}\right) + \left(\frac{18 \times 10\ 000}{820\ 000}\right)$$

$$\text{new index} = \quad 0.117 \quad + \quad 0.439 \quad + \quad 0.424 \quad + \quad 0.220$$

$$= \quad 1.20$$

Multiplying this by our indexing factor of 1000 we get a new level of 1200, 20 per cent up on the original 1000. Although in this example we have chosen to increase the value of all our stocks by 20 per cent in order to illustrate how the index will rise, under realistic circumstances some stocks will be going down while others will be going up. Whichever the direction, on a penny for penny move, the highest capitalization stocks, B and C in our example, will have the greatest effect.

A general formula for the calculation of a capitalization-weighted index is as follows:

$$\frac{\sum_{r=1}^{N} Nr\ Pr}{B}$$

where:

N is the number of index constituents
Nr is the number of shares issued in constituent company r
Pr is the price of the company r
B is the original base capitalization

Comparison of Dow Jones to the S & P 500

It might be supposed that the Dow Jones when compared to the S & P 500 would give a very different view of the overall market. We are, after all, setting a 30 share arithmetic mean against a 500 share capitalization-weighted index. The surprise in fact comes when we see just how well the two indices track each other.

In Figure 2.1 both indices have been rebased to a level of 100 for

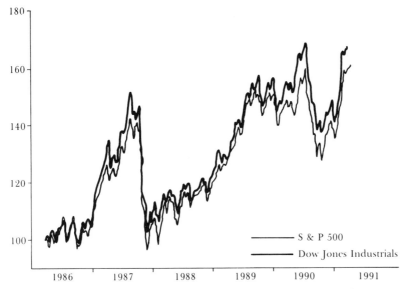

Figure 2.1   Comparison of performance, Dow Jones Industrials to
S & P 500

the start of 1986; by the early part of 1991 the Dow Jones has only risen about five points more than the S & P 500 on this scale, and the general movement over the period has been very close. The five points differential translates to an approximate overperformance of 3 per cent by the Dow Jones over the S & P 500 for the period.

Geometric averages and the Value Line Composite Index

Although the Value Line 1700 Index was the first stock index to have a futures contract, its history is far more recent than that of the Dow Jones or S & P 500. Arnold Bernhard & Co started calculating and publishing the Value Line Composite Index initially as a means of monitoring its own performance in stock selection. But the breadth of the index, with its 1700 stocks and representing over 95 per cent of the capitalization of all US equities, soon brought it to prominence as an even better indicator in many ways than the Dow or the S & P 500. As the Value Line includes many second-line stocks in addition to the blue-chips, it is a very much more volatile index than the S & P 500, but this is also in part due to the way that the Value Line Composite Index is calculated. It is an equally weighted geometric average of its constituent stocks. This means that each stock represents approximately 1/1700th of the index.

The formula used in calculating a geometric average is:

$n\sqrt{}$the product of n stock prices

so if we had just 3 stocks with prices of 2, 3 and 4 the geometric average would be

$3\sqrt{2 \times 3 \times 4} = 3\sqrt{24} = 2.89$

In order to calculate the index we first divide each stock's closing price by the previous day's closing price. The price changes of all the stocks are then averaged geometrically and the resulting figure is multiplied by the preceding day's closing Value Line Composite Index. If yesterday's closing price of the index was 150.83 and the geometric mean of today's price changes is calculated to be 1.021, then today's index close would be:

$150.83 \times 1.021 = 154.00$

The base of the index was defined to be 100 on 30 June 1961.

As with the Dow Jones, because the index is not capitalization-weighted adjustments have to be made for stock splits. This is done by adjusting the previous day's closing price for the split or divided change making it equivalent to a post split price. The new index is then computed to this 'new' yesterday's closing price. Because of the large number of stocks in this index, additions of new stocks and deletions tend to have almost no effect on the overall index.

Today the index is calculated continuously throughout the trading day. Value Line Investment Survey also computes indices on approximately 1500 industrial stocks to give an Industrial Average, as well as a Railroad Average and Utility Average; but for our purposes only the Value Line Composite Index is important as that is the index used by the Kansas City Board of Trade for its futures contract.

Comparisons and differences

We have looked at the main ways of calculating indices but have not so far considered whether one is better than another. In many ways the question 'which index is the best?' is pointless. The Dow Jones can be argued to be out of date because it is far too narrow to reflect the market truly. On the other hand, it has been around for a long time and is still used as a guide by all investors remotely interested in the American stock markets. Certainly the S & P 500 can be considered to be more representative of market activity, but in that case why is the more sophisticated Value Line Composite Index with its 1700 shares not more widely accepted—particularly as the first stock index futures contract was based on it? While the 1700 or so equities that make up the Value Line may sometimes cause greater volatility to the index, in part this is offset by the dampening effect of using a geometric average. Possibly the ideal would be to construct a capitalization-weighted geometric average index based on all stocks traded on American stock exchanges. The question would then remain—would anyone pay any attention to it? We come back to the rather unscientific conclusion that the 'best' index is the one that people look at the most because in some way they relate to it, and are happy to use it.

Other American indices

As well as the Dow Jones, S & P 500 and the Value Line Composite, there are other indices used in the USA that one should be aware of.

The New York Stock Exchange Composite Index

The NYSE Index is a capitalization-weighted index calculated similarly to the S & P 500 but is much broader based in that it encompasses all of the 1400 (approximately) stocks listed on the NYSE. A base of 50 was set for the original index on 31 December 1965 as that figure was close to the average share price of shares traded on the NYSE at that time. Because of the very strict listing requirements for companies on the NYSE, the NYSE has more than its fair share of all the blue-chip stocks traded on various American stock markets. It is thus a useful index for funds heavily weighted to investing in the blue-chip stocks, less useful for an investor seeking to trade a high volatility index.

Table 2.2   Stocks in the MMI

American Express	IBM
AT & T	International Paper
Chevron	Johnson & Johnson
Coca-Cola	Merck & Co
Dow Chemical	Minnesota Mining & Mfg
Du Pont	Mobil
Eastman Kodak	Philip Morris
Exxon	Procter & Gamble
General Electric	Sears Roebuck
General Motors	USX

The Major Market Index (MMI)

The Major Market Index is traded as a futures contract on the CBOT, but as an option on the American Stock Exchange (AMEX), and gets some of its kudos from the fact that the MMI starts to trade 15 minutes before the Dow Jones and S & P 500 open their quotations. It, therefore, has a 15-minute period when it is the dominant indicator of how the American markets may open. It is based on just 20 blue-chip stocks, generally the largest and internationally most known corporations of the American stock markets. Unlike most other indices, it is not capitalization-weighted being calculated as an equally weighted price index. Prices used to calculate the index are those trading on the NYSE, not the AMEX.

With currently 17 of the MMI stocks in the Dow Jones, and a similar method of calculation, it is little wonder that sometimes the MMI is referred to as a 'proxy for the Dow' which, bearing in mind the history of the MMI, is rather ironic. Correlation between the two contracts is unsurprisingly close at 97 per cent. The current list of stocks on the MMI is shown in Table 2.2.

Oil Stock Index (XOI)

The Oil Stock Index is a little different to other indices that we have looked at as it represents only one industrial sector, not the market as a whole. The unique nature of the oil sector often means that the market generally may be doing one thing while the 'oils' are doing something entirely different. The index itself is a capitalization-weighted index based on 30 leading US companies involved in oil and gas production. As a specific sector index it allows investors to take an isolated investment view and so either increase gearing just in this sector, or hedge out of a broad portfolio particular near-term risks that may be perceived in the oil sector.

Computer Stock Index

The Computer Stock Index is again a capitalization-weighted index made up of 30 leading US high technology stocks and useful to the investor wishing to manage investment risks in this sector more efficiently. The one drawback to this index is that IBM accounts for just over half of the capitalization, making it a little 'imbalanced'.

Different exchanges

With the developing cross-market contract fungibility that we see today, one particular index contract may be traded in different exchanges. We have already noted that the MMI future is traded on the CBOT while the option is traded on the American Stock Exchange, as well as on the European Options Exchange (EOE) in Amsterdam. The New York Stock Exchange Composite trades a future and options contract on the New York Futures Exchange, while the New York Stock Exchange trades a smaller NYSE Composite options contract ($100 × index instead of the $500 × index on the NYFE). Contract fungibility, both domestic and international, is growing. A list of all current stock index futures and options contracts and their locations is given in Appendix 2.

European stock indices

We shall now look at all the more important European stock indices, which while reflecting much of the historical development seen in the US market are nevertheless quite unique. As well as the immediate problem of each index relating to share prices in different currencies, each is also the product of differing cultural as well as economic backgrounds.

The UK FT 30, All Share and FT-SE 100

The FT 30 Index, first published in 1935, is calculated as the geometric average of 30 major industrial companies. Although the constituents of the index are updated to try to make it as representative of 'the market' as possible, and the index is now calculated on a real-time basis, it still only accounts for some 30 per cent of market capitalization. Also, as it is based on geometric averaging in the long run it is likely to underperform more broadly defined arithmetic average based indices. It is still, however, used by many investors as a guide to what is happening in the market—particularly by those investors who were trading at a time when the FT 30 Index was the only guide to what was happening in the UK market!

In order to have more representative monitors of the stock market, the Financial Times Actuaries indices were introduced in 1962. These indices survey various sectors of the market, while the FTA All Share Index provides a measure of the market as a whole. The FTA All Share is a capitalization-weighted arithmetic average index based on over 700 equities and covering over 90 per cent of the total UK market capitalization. It has come to be regarded as the benchmark index for the UK market. The performance of portfolios, as well as that of the fund managers, is judged by comparison with the performance of the FTA All Share.

With the development of the London International Financial Futures Exchange (LIFFE) and the London Traded Options Market (LTOM), both of whom wished to trade a stock index contract, it became necessary to develop a new index more suited to this requirement. The FT 30 was too narrowly based to be representative of the market, and consequently of little use for investment or portfolio hedging, while the All Share was regarded as too broad to provide the rapid indication and calculation of market movement that traders and arbitrageurs require. The new index that addressed these problems was the Financial Times-Stock Exchange 100, or FT-SE 100.

This first UK real-time index, recalculated every minute of the trading day, was launched in January 1984. As the name suggests, the FT-SE 100 Index is based on the equities of 100 of the largest UK quoted companies, and is calculated as a capitalization-weighted arithmetic average. The 100 companies that make up the

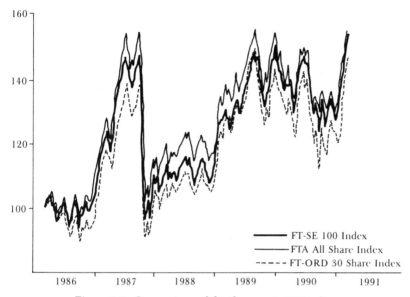

160 ┐

140 ┤

120 ┤

100 ┤

FT-SE 100 Index
FTA All Share Index
FT-ORD 30 Share Index

1986   1987   1988   1989   1990   1991

Figure 2.2 Comparison of the three main UK indices

index account for almost 70 per cent of the capitalization of the entire UK equity market, and as such there is a close correlation with the FTA All Share Index, about 98 per cent.

Figure 2.2, which compares the three UK indices where all are rebased to the same point for the start of 1986, shows a fairly consistent ranking for the five-year period. Best performance is seen by the FTA All Share Index, traditionally explained by the growth of the many smaller companies that the All Share Index captures, and that are not seen in the other two indices. For the opposite reason we are not surprised to see the FT-ORD 30 Share Index as the poorest performer, comprising as it does well-established blue-chips that will at best grow in line with the national economy.

Figure 2.3, however, throws this assumption into a little confusion, and illustrates the problem of using such charts in order to determine which index performs 'best'. It compares just the FT-SE 100 Index with the FT-ORD 30 Share, but is taken five years further back. We now see the FT-ORD 30 as the consistently better performer. Clearly, index-performance comparisons can only be regarded as snapshots over a known time period; there is no universal reason as to why one index should always perform

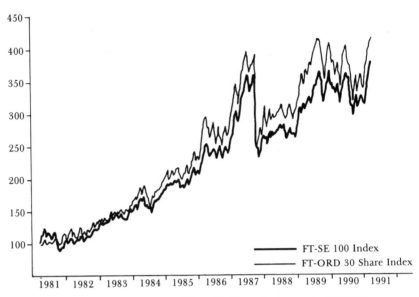

Figure 2.3 Comparison of the FT-SE 100 Index to the FT-ORD
Index over 10 years

better or worse than another. While a larger based index should
show better market growth, in uncertain times blue-chip shares
will attract investment (or lack of selling) as nervous investors
prefer to stick to quality. The FT-SE 100 Index is influenced by a
further factor that does not affect the FT-ORD 30 or the All Share
to as large a degree, that of compositional change. Changes of
constituents to the FT-ORD 30 are rare; the All Share is so
encompassing that changes are constant but rather peripheral.
With the 100 Share Index, based on 100 of the most highly
capitalized companies in the UK we can see a trend that has
altered the compositional nature of the index. When the index was
established in 1984, the decline of the UK's manufacturing base
was already underway, and the inclusion of more service and
financial companies in the index, as the size of manufacturing firms
diminished, was expected. With the progress of the UK
government's privatization programme, the index has now taken
on a 'utility' bias; it is certainly not representing the same type of
constituents that made up the FT-SE 100 Index in 1984. However,
it still remains representative of the 100 most highly capitalized

companies in the country and is much more of a dynamic index than the other two major UK indices.

In order to ensure that the FT-SE 100 Index remains up-to-date, the constituents are selected from a list of 120 of the highest capitalized UK companies. A 'Steering Committee' meets at least quarterly to review the index constituents and if necessary to make changes so as to keep the index representative of the largest companies in the UK market.

France and the CAC-40 Index

The French International Futures and Options Market, known as the MATIF, opened in February 1986 with a futures long-bond contract. Since that time several other futures and options contracts have been introduced, reflecting the spectacular growth of this industry in France. If not in actual contract types then certainly in traded volume, the MATIF has become a serious rival to the London International Financial Future Exchange.

On 15 June 1988 the Paris Bourse introduced the CAC-40 Stock Index, an index based on a representative sample of 40 stocks traded on the Monthly Settlement Market (Règlement Mensuel-RM). Stocks were chosen to represent all the major economic sectors of the French market (Table 2.3). In 1987 retrospective analysis showed that these 40 stocks had a market capitalization of some 63 per cent of the French equity market, but some 70 per cent of traded volume.

The index is capitalization-weighted and was set to a base value of 1000 on 31 December 1987. It is continuously calculated from 10 am to 5 pm, new index levels being 'published' every 30 seconds to the various information systems. As a back-up, an 'éclaireur' or 'guide' system replaces the index when accurate calculation is not possible. This provides a 'best available' guide to the index level at times when not all of the CAC-40 equities have yet traded, such as at the beginning of the day, and at rare times when because of exceptional circumstances the proper calculation cannot be performed.

Based on the CAC-40 Index, the MATIF launched its stock index futures contract in November 1988 and traded in the open outcry market.

At the same time, MONEP introduced an American-style

Table 2.3   Stocks of the CAC-40 Index

Accor	Havas
Arjomari-Prioux	Lafarge Coppee
Air Liquide	Legrand
BSN	LVMH
Bancaire	Lyonnaise des Eaux
Bouygues	Matra
CGE	Merlin Gerin
CGIP	Michelin
Canal Plus	Midi
Cap Gemini Sogeti	L'Oreal
Carrefour	Paribas
Casino	Pernod Ricard
Chargeurs SA	Peugeot
Club Med	St Gobain
Credit Commercial	St Louis
Credit Foncier	Sanofi
Dumez	Societe Generale
Elf Aquitaine	Suez
General des Eaux	Thomason-CSF
Hachette	UAP

options contract on the CAC-40. MONEP, Marché des Options Negociables de Paris, is the French stock and index options market and while a newer market than the MATIF, having commenced trading only on 10 September 1987, has also exhibited considerable growth in liquidity and open interest. MONEP is located inside the Paris Palais de la Bourse.

The MATIF and MONEP coordinated the CAC-40 futures and options contracts so that both have the same contract size, trading months, expiry, trading hours and margins (a salutary lesson for the London market where after six years this is just starting to be considered).

The Dutch and their stock index contracts

Europe's first options exchange was established in Amsterdam in 1978, and being the first it naturally called itself the European Options Exchange (EOE). With its innovative approach, it was the first exchange in the world to introduce gold, bond and currency options as well as arranging tie-ups with other exchanges around the world. In 1987, the EOE was able to introduce an option on the American Major Market Index, a contract fully fungible with that traded on AMEX in New York. Growth in these various contracts has been dramatic. With a start of 1000 or so contracts a day in 1978, the EOE now trades over 55 000 contracts a day.

The first index options contract to be introduced by the EOE came in May 1987, and was based on the weighted average of 25 representative blue-chip stocks of the Amsterdam Stock Exchange. In the same year, on the initiative of the EOE, the Amsterdam Financial Futures Market (FTA) started its operations. This led to the introduction, by August 1988, of a futures contract on the EOE stock index. EOE stock index options and futures contracts are identical in make-up and expiry, and are designed to be traded so as to augment each other.

In 1989, the EOE introduced a new stock index contract, the Dutch TOP5. This index is made up of five of the most liquid and largest stocks on the Amsterdam Stock Exchange as well as being traded on other leading exchanges in Europe and the USA. These five stocks used in the TOP5 Index are: Akzo, KLM, Philips, Royal Dutch and Unilever, and the index is based on a system that assumes equal investment in each stock as at the end of 1989. The level of the TOP5 Index can, therefore, be calculated by multiplying the share prices by the appropriate weighting factor and then dividing the sum of these calculations by 100. Futures and options contracts were introduced at the same time, the future being traded on the FTA and the European style TOP5 option on the EOE. As can be expected, both contracts are identical with regard to size, trading periods and expiry.

Scandinavian index contracts

Denmark
Options and futures started trading in 1987, initially by the open outcry method. After two years, this was changed in January 1989 to a decentralized electronic trading system. Trading may still be done outside the electronic system, but any such trades have to be promptly reported for registration.

The Copenhagen Stock Exchange officially lists contracts that can be traded and these, therefore, come under the jurisdiction of

the Danish Guarantee Fund. This fund, established by the leading
Danish financial institutions, acts as a clearing house and admin-
isters the rules of trading so as to 'guarantee' the performance of
the exchange.

Both index futures and index options contracts are available, the
futures contract being based on the KFX stock index, an index
comprising 25 leading stocks of the Copenhagen Stock Exchange.
The options contract is a European-style option on the KFX stock
index future. Stock inclusions are revised quarterly.

Finland
Both options and futures contracts are traded, based on the 25
most traded stocks on the Helsinki Stock Exchange, but these are
not available for international trading—they are purely domestic
products. FOX, the Finnish Options Index, is a European style
option.

Norway
The Norwegian Options Market trades the OBX, an index options
contract based on the 25 most actively traded stocks on the Oslo
Stock Exchange. It includes Norsk Hydro, one of the most actively
traded stocks on any Scandinavian Market in recent years.

Sweden
The Stockholm Options Market, OM, was established in 1985 and
now trades a range of equity options as well as several other
financial instruments. One of the great Scandinavian success
stories has been the spectacular growth of the OMX index options
contract, presently one of the most actively traded index options
contracts outside the USA. Volumes are averaging 18 000
contracts per day. The options contract is European in style and is
based on 30 of the most active stocks in the Swedish market. The
OM is available for trading by foreign investors, while the index
futures contract is available only to domestic investors. The market
itself is a fully automated electronic screen-based system, complete
with integrated clearing and settlement.

The Swedish 'Exchange' in London
Because of the success of the Swedish stock market in attracting
overseas involvement in their derivative products, OM London

Ltd (OML) was established in December 1989 as a means of further promoting their activities. OML is a wholly owned subsidiary of OM Gruppen AB and acts as an electronic order matching exchange and integrated clearing house. It is linked on a real-time basis to the Swedish derivatives market, OM in Stockholm, and for the instruments that are traded both in London and Stockholm this creates one market place with combined liquidity, open interest and the best market price, whether arising in London or Stockholm.

As well as being able to use OML to trade certain Swedish and Norwegian stock options, OMX (Index) options and futures are also available to traders wishing to use the London–Stockholm electronic link, as are GEMX options and futures, OM London's German Equity Market Index.

GEMX has been designed to provide a good proxy for the German equity market and is made up of 20 major stocks trading on the Frankfurt Stock Exchange. Correlation with the DAX is close, which nevertheless must be regarded as the better proxy for the German equity market, being made up of 30 stocks. All but one of the GEMX stocks are included in the DAX.

Whether the GEMX contracts can continue to attract investors against the DAX traded in Germany remains to be seen. Singapore still manages to attract a small but healthy interest on its Nikkei Index contract against the might of all the other index contracts traded in Japan. Whatever the success of one contract against another, the OML concept is one worth noting. A 'market place' no longer needs to have a specific location, or any location at all for that matter. Electronic links can be created between any so-called market locations in order to boost liquidity and create a more efficient market. As specifically in the case of OM, it is also an elegant way of promoting a domestic equity market to a greater degree of international exposure. Whether many such links will be developed in the near future, however, remains in doubt. The very high level of equity information provided by international quotational screen-based systems, together with the fact that most large brokers have access to overseas offices, often at the touch of a button, gives the impression that more electronic link-ups would simply result in a duplication of facilities. A trader in Hong Kong wishing to trade a European index will have little interest whether the contract is booked in Dublin, Amsterdam or Warsaw, so long

as the contract he wishes to trade is liquid and representative of
the market that he views.

Switzerland

The Swiss Options and Financial Futures Exchange, known more
commonly as SOFFEX, commenced trading in May 1988. Initially, only stock options were traded, but by the end of the same
year an option on the Swiss Market Index (SMI) had been
introduced. The SMI is a capitalization-weighted index based on
24 of the most significant stocks traded on the Basel, Geneva and
Zürich Stock Exchanges. Every time the price of any of the stocks
change, the index is automatically recalculated. The proportion of
index options contracts to other stock options contracts oscillates
between one third and over half of all business done. Of particular
interest is the fact that SOFFEX was one of the first fully
computerized screen trading and clearing markets.

Germany: the DTB and the DAX

For various historical reasons Germany has been rather slower at
developing a financial futures and options market than the other
European countries. Following the depression and the hyperinfla-
tion of the 1920s, futures markets were abolished in 1931 and
futures and options trading was prohibited by law. Increasing
stock market activity during the 1960s led to demands for the
reintroduction of options contracts, and finally in 1970 the stock
options market was re-established. Unfortunately, the market
growth was somewhat hampered by the requirement that options
contracts were subject to the country's gaming laws. One spurious
benefit of this was that investors, other than registered dealers,
could choose not to honour their debts! As a result, for the
protection of dealers, margin requirements on investors became so
absurdly high as to negate most of the benefits of options usage.
Only with the evident success of other European options and
financial futures markets during the latter part of the 1980s were
the German authorities persuaded to enact legislation that would
allow them to develop a 'proper' options and futures market.
Action was greatly speeded up when the LIFFE launched its Bund
contract in September 1988 (since proved to be one of the LIFFE's
most successful contracts).

Table 2.4 Stocks of the DAX Index

Allianz	Karstadt
BASF	Kaufhof
BMW	Linde
Bayer	Lufthansa
Bayerische Hypo	MAN AG
Bayerische Vereins	Mannesmann
Commerzbank	Metallgesellschaft
Continental	Preussag
Daimler-Benz	RWE
Degussa	Schering
Deutsche Babcock	Siemens
Deutsche Bank	Thyssen
Dresdner Bank	Veba
Henkel	VAGA
Hoechst	Volkswagen

Having created the necessary legislation, the DTB Deutsche Terminbörse GmbH was set up in July 1988 as a company owned by 17 leading German financial institutions. These include leading commercial and private banks as well as savings institutions, and under their auspices the DTB now operates as Germany's options and futures exchange. Contracts are now available in over 20 stock options, a Bund future and the DAX stock index future. The market itself is an electronic market with computer-based trading and clearing, without any actual trading floor.

The Deutscher Aktienindex (DAX)

This DAX is made up of 30 major German companies that represent approximately 60 per cent of the total capitalization of the German market and account for over 65 per cent of the trading volume on the stock exchange (Table 2.4).

A peculiarity of the DAX is that although capitalization-weighted, it is calculated as a 'Performance Index', all dividends and bonus shares are accumulated in the index. The reason for this is that as dividends on the German stock market are concentrated into just May, June and July, if dividends were not reinvested, the index might not give an accurate indication of the performance of the market.

The DAX is calculated every minute during the official trading hours of the Frankfurt Stock Exchange, the country's largest. It is worth noting that the Frankfurt Stock Exchange is only one of eight German exchanges although it does handle about 65 per cent of all stock volume. Moves by the Frankfurt Exchange to channel all blue-chip equity trading through Frankfurt are naturally being resisted by the smaller exchanges. At present the outcome of such moves is uncertain, particularly with the chance of new companies emerging once the old East German economy starts to catch up. The betting, however, must be that volume is attracted to existing volume and liquidity, and that the Frankfurt Exchange will gradually become even more dominant.

Japanese stock index derivatives

The 'modern' Japanese Stock Exchanges were established in 1949 in Tokyo, Osaka and Nagoya, and although other stock exchanges were later set up in several other major cities, the Tokyo Exchange remains the largest with over 75 per cent of all Japanese stock exchange transactions. Growth of activity on these exchanges has been such that total volumes traded at present rival traded volumes (in value) of the American exchanges.

At the same time as the modern Japanese stock exchanges were being created, the Nikkei Stock Average came into being, on 16 May 1949. It is managed by Nihon Keisai Shimbun Inc, Japan's foremost business newspaper group and calculated every minute as the arithmetic mean of the 225 underlying stocks listed on the Tokyo Stock Exchange. It is not capitalization-weighted, but is based on the adjustment method as used by the Dow-Jones. The 225 stocks that make up the Nikkei Stock Average account for over 70 per cent in trading volume and about 55 per cent of the total capitalization of the First Section stocks listed on the Tokyo Exchange.

SIMEX and the Nikkei futures contract

Because of the peculiar difficulties that had to be overcome before stock index contracts could be traded in Japan, the Nikkei futures contract was first launched on the Singapore International Monetary Exchange (SIMEX) in 1986, following an agreement between the Chicago Mercantile Exchange (CME) and Nihon

Keisai Shimbun Inc, which allowed the CME to introduce the contract on SIMEX (with which the CME has mutual offset arrangements). Although the contract enjoyed considerable success in its early days, with the introduction of stock index contracts in Japan, it has now rather declined.

The Osaka 50 Index

It was only in June 1987 that Japan was able to introduce its own 'domestic' stock index contract. As the legal constraints of not being able to trade contracts without a physical delivery had not yet been reconciled, the Osaka 50 Index futures contract was designed to accept or give physical delivery of the underlying stock on expiry.

Because calculation of the number of shares of each of the constituent elements, required on delivery, was a peculiarly complex chore, very few contracts were taken to delivery. The Osaka Securities Exchange (OSE) could, nevertheless, boast a 'first' and successful stock index futures contract. One other specific problem encountered with this contract, a result of the stock delivery requirement, was its very large size, the underlying value being some ¥55 million or about US$ 400 000, very much a contract only for the professional investor.

With the introduction of cash-settled stock index futures in Japan, the Osaka 50 has declined in trading volume to such an extent that its long-term future must be uncertain. It remains, however, an interesting example of Japanese ingenuity in the face of Japanese bureaucracy, and in its early days was a very successful index contract.

Within a year of the OSE 50 starting to trade, the Japanese government passed legislation that allowed the settlement of index futures to be in cash. As a result, on 3 September 1988 the OSE introduced the Nikkei 225 futures contract, and the Tokyo Stock Exchange started trading in futures on their TOPIX Index.

The Nikkei 225 futures contract is based on the same index that is used by SIMEX for their Nikkei 225 futures contract. There are two main differences: the Osaka contract is twice as big, 1000 yen times the index as opposed to 500 yen for the SIMEX contract; and the Osaka contract is traded on a screen-based matching trades system—SIMEX trades by open outcry. Volume on the Osaka contract has grown spectacularly, far outpacing that on the

Singapore market, and starting to be comparable with volumes traded by the S & P 500.

TOPIX

The Tokyo Stock Exchange (TSE) introduced their TOPIX Index in July of 1969 as a replacement for a Dow-based index calculation. TOPIX is calculated each minute, and is a capitalization-weighted arithmetic mean of the underlying shares of the First Section of the Tokyo Stock Market. This First Section is made up of established stocks with substantial capitalizations, and can be readily traded. The total number of stocks in this section is 1138. Newer companies with smaller capitalizations and less liquid shares are consigned to the 'Second Section' of the Tokyo Stock Market, but the TSE regularly reviews stocks in both sections in order to maintain the status of the first and second divisions by promoting or demoting suitable equities. Both the Nikkei 225 and the TOPIX contract now have options contracts, both of which are screen-traded. More recently, agreement was finalized to allow the Nikkei 225 and the TOPIX futures and options to be traded in Chicago—another step in the progressive globalization of derivatives markets.

Although the bulk of Japanese index futures and options volume is held by the Nikkei 225 contracts in Osaka, the TOPIX contract, nevertheless, trades a very respectable amount and is favoured by those who claim it is more representative of the Japanese equity markets. The stocks of the Nikkei 225 account for only about 55 per cent of the total capitalization of TOPIX, which, logically, has a far greater proportion of many smaller companies than the Nikkei 225. As the Nikkei is not a capitalization-weighted index, large priced shares have a big effect on the index, which is not seen on TOPIX. This difference is also apparent when stocks that have not traded for some time suddenly trade at significantly different levels to those previously (both indices are calculated on last traded prices). The movement of the Nikkei 225 will then be larger than the change on TOPIX.

Relative performance of TOPIX and the Nikkei 225

As all indices are designed for a specific function, it is a matter of value judgement to determine what should be regarded as the 'base'. If we regard the base as the FTA World Index Japanese

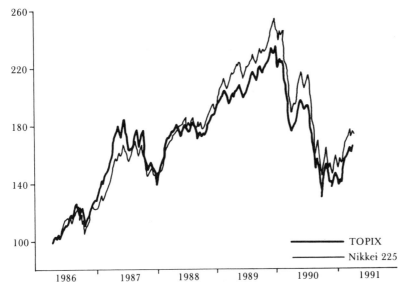

Figure 2.4 Comparison of TOPIX and Nikkei 225

sector, we would expect in any comparison to see that the Nikkei 225, with its smaller number of stocks and not being capitalization-weighted, to show the greatest divergence from the FTA World Index Japanese sector, and indeed this is what can be observed.

A comparison of the Nikkei 225 to TOPIX with both indices rebased to 100 for the start of 1986 surprisingly shows an early outperformance by TOPIX, but from 1988 onwards a fairly consistent outperformance of the non-weighted Nikkei 225 (Table 2.4). The retrospective view also puts into perspective just how little the Japanese markets were affected by the crash of October 1987, and how much more serious was the Japanese's own decline of 1989/90.

Settlement
One of the peculiarities of the Japanese market is that settlement of open positions on futures contracts is not at the closing price at contract expiry, but at the opening prices of the underlying stocks that make up the index, on the day after contract expiry. This can result in a significant difference being seen between index closing levels and actual settlement levels.

Other trading restrictions

The Japanese regulatory authorities have decided that the maximum fall or rise in any one day should be limited to about 3 per cent of the value of the index. For the futures contracts, the Daily Price Limit Movement is taken from the previous day's closing level. The same rule applies to the options markets.

A further market control is exercised by the 'Saitori' or 'Nakadachi' members of Tokyo and Osaka respectively. These market members have the discretion to act as intermediaries between traders in order to decrease the speed with which the market is moving, when directed to do so by the regulatory authorities.

Activities of this nature may have the effect of giving the appearance of a more orderly market, while in practice it is still impossible for a large panic seller to unload his position. The pain just lasts longer, but some of the screaming is avoided.

It is also worth bearing in mind that some of the Nikkei 225 stocks are fairly illiquid, and as the index is not capitalization-weighted, such stocks, where they have a large percentage of the index, could be used to manipulate the index at important times such as expiry.

CHAPTER 3

Pricing of stock index futures

General relationships of forward prices

When dealing with stock index futures contracts the most fundamental concept that we have to appreciate is that of 'fair-value'.
All forward, or futures, contracts have a theoretical relationship
with the prompt or cash value of the traded item, and this
theoretical forward price is defined as the fair-value of the forward
contract.

Perhaps the simplest futures market pricing mechanism to
understand is that affecting gold. Gold produces no yield, and if
we assume storage and insurance costs of zero then the cost of
holding gold is purely the cost of finance, i.e. the money that we
would have earned if instead of buying gold we had put our money
on deposit. So, with spot gold at US\$ 400 and financing rates of
say 11 per cent, the cost of carry for our gold for three months
would be:

$$400 \times \frac{11}{100} \times \frac{3}{12} = \$11$$

thus three months gold should be trading at US\$ 411, its fair-value
(Figure 3.1). If interest rates change, the cost of carry will change
accordingly. For shorter or longer periods the correct forward price
can be calculated, and would show a relationship as on the graph.

For a single interest rate the graph will show a straight line; a
different interest rate, and the line will show a different slope. Life,
however, is never quite so simple. Forward interest rates can be
different for different points in the future. They may be 10⅞ per

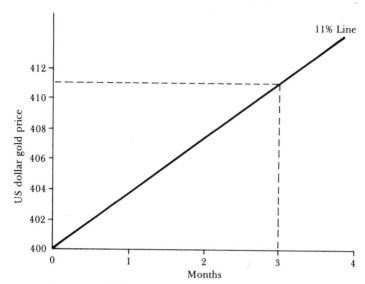

Figure 3.1   Three months gold trading at its fair-value

cent for two months, 11 per cent for three months, $11\frac{1}{16}$ per cent for four months and may be $10^{15}\!/_{16}$ for six months consequently our graph in reality should show a curve with a flattening top (Fig 3.2).

It is also worth bearing in mind that the cost of financing is not a universal cost. The rate at which a private individual may borrow money will regrettably be considerably less advantageous than rates available to BP, ICI or Daimler Benz; fair-value calculations should, therefore, be fine-tuned to the specific rates available to particular market participants, although in practice the small differences thus seen will only be of interest to arbitrageurs.

All physical commodities will have a theoretical futures price based on an interest rate cost of carry; for cheaper metals like copper or zinc, as well as the soft commodities, costs of storage become more significant and need to be taken in the calculation.

Forward prices of physical commodities will rarely rise much above their theoretical futures prices; whenever they do, an arbitrage profit can be made by buying the cash or prompt (with borrowed funds) and selling the futures contract against it. When the futures contract expires, the cash position is delivered and a return greater than the financing cost (plus storage and insurance if necessary) is realized. As a matter of course many financial institutions are constantly on the look-out for such opportunities—which is why they don't often occur, and when they do, they usually do not last for any great length of time.

There may be a limit on how much the forward price of a physical commodity can rise above the cash, but there is no such limit in the other direction. If market forces conspire to create a nearby shortage then the price of the prompt commodity can rise and rise, far above that of the forward price. Speculating on this 'backwardation' to disappear, selling a highly priced nearby date and buying a cheap forward date may appear an attractive gamble. However, backwardations have the very nasty habit of increasing far beyond logic and expectation, particularly when someone may be trying to corner the market, and lasting far longer than any original estimates. Backwardations in the metal markets have been known to last for years.

Fair-value of stock index futures

Forward pricing of stock indices is a little more involved than that seen in the previous gold example but the general definition still holds good (Figure 3.2). If we buy a commodity or a cash stock portfolio with borrowed funds and sell its fairly valued futures contract against it there will be no arbitrage profit or loss.

Stock indices are different from gold or other physical commodites in that the constituents of the index generate a yield by way of dividends, so if we buy the 100 constituent stocks of the FT-SE 100 Index with borrowed funds, our cost of carry is reduced by the dividends paid to us as owners of the stock. If we assume a financing rate of 11 per cent and an average stock yield of 4.5 per cent from the constituents of the FT-SE 100 Index, then at an index level of 2400 we can calculate the 'fair-difference' or 'basis' between the spot index and its futures contract with, say, three months to expiry as follows:

$$\text{financing costs} = 2400 \times \frac{11}{100} \times \frac{3}{12} = 66 \text{ points}$$

$$\text{dividend paid} = 2400 \times \frac{4.5}{100} \times \frac{3}{12} = 27 \text{ points}$$

Basis, therefore, is 39 points, so fair-value for the future would be 2439.

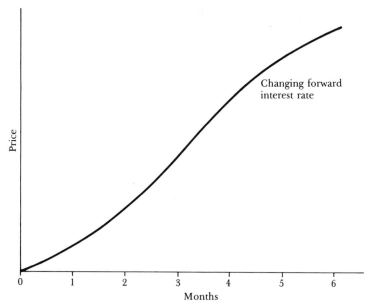

Changing forward
interest rate

Figure 3.2   Forward pricing of stock indices

We can, therefore, define a simple formula for the calculation of 'basis', for the fair-value premium thus:

simple formula for fair-value premium

$$F = I \times \left[\frac{(i - y)}{100} \times \frac{d}{365} \right]$$

where F = fair-value premium or basis
       I = FT-SE 100 Index level
       i = interest rate over d days
       y = percentage yield on index
       d = days in the funding period

Since dividend yields are usually less than financing costs, there is a net cost of carry, and the future should, therefore, trade at a premium to cash.

The simple formula for the fair-value premium outlined above is really only useful as a quick and rough guide. It is severely limited by two major factors: settlement anomalies and uneven dividend flow. In London, the International Stock Exchange (ISE) accounts in two-week and occasionally three-week (at Christmas, etc.) periods. Consequently, stock purchases must be financed between the settlement date of the current ISE account and the settlement

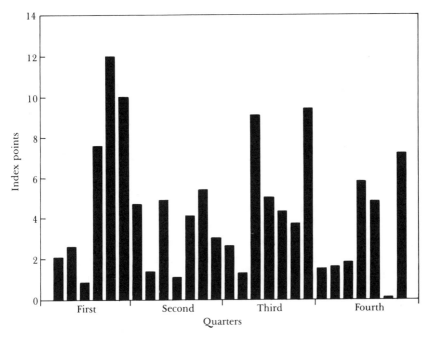

Figure 3.3 Expected dividend flow

date of the ISE account in which the futures contract expires. A far trickier problem for us to consider is that presented by the uneven flow of dividends throughout the year.

Figure 3.3 shows the distribution of expected dividends during 1991, and is shown in index points when the index stands at 2550 and broken down by accounting periods. By quarter we might expect to receive the following totalled dividends (with the index at 2550):

Quarter	Points	% yield
1	35.2	1.38
2	24.6	.97
3	35.4	1.39
4	22.8	.89
Total	118.0	4.63

Although the annual yield comes to 4.63 per cent we see that a large portion of this dividend actually falls in the first and third quarters of the year.

In this example we have used index points as they give us a

direct insight on how the futures contract fair-value will be affected. The initial calculation is, however, derived from the total percentage dividend paid on the 100 Share Index, and is then broken down into constituent ISE accounting periods.

Periods of higher dividend returns, such as the first quarter of the year, will correspond to periods when the major constituents of the FT-SE 100 Index (BP, Telecom, Shell) pay their dividends. Allowance for these distortions from the 4.63 per cent yield norm is easy enough to compute, but even this involves a considerable degree of 'judgement' as dividends are not known with certainty in advance of their publication. The best that we can do is to take last year's dividends and increase them by say 10 per cent as a starting point. Then ongoing adjustments can be made as dividend trends become established in similar industries, and as they are seen to be affected by economic factors or unique factors affecting specific companies. A final conundrum that will affect calculations is that of dividend timing. We may know that a particular company pays its dividend at the end of June but the exact payment date may not be known until some time in May. Our fair-value calculation for the June futures contract which is worked out in early April will, therefore, have an 'uncertainty factor' depending on whether the dividend is paid in one account or the next—which in this case will be under the next quarterly futures contract.

Bearing in mind the aforementioned constraints we can now improve our formula for the calculation of fair-value premium as follows:

improved fair-value premium formula

$$F = I \times \left[\left(\frac{i}{100} - \frac{d}{365}\right) - \left(\frac{y}{100} \times \frac{p}{P}\right)\right]$$

where p = dividend payments expected between now and the expiry of the contract

P = the total dividend payments expected in the full year ending on the expiry of the futures contract

It is as well to remember that although earlier we calculated a fair-value premium to be a certain number of points, the premium is actually a percentage of the index. In a rapidly rising or declining market where large moves have been seen this will become a significant factor.

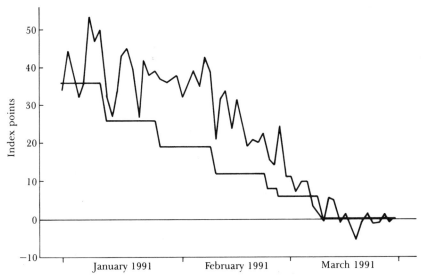

Figure 3.4   FT-SE 100 Index March 1991 futures contract (simple and theoretical basis)

fair-value premium % $= \text{(finance-dividend)} \times \text{time}$

$\qquad\qquad\qquad\qquad = 11\% - 4.5\% \times \frac{3}{12}$

$\qquad\qquad\qquad\qquad = 1.625\% \text{ per quarter}$

at 2400 fair-value premium $= 39$ points

at 2650 fair-value premium $= 43$ points

A simple chart of fair-value premium over the life of a quarterly futures contract will show fair-value premium declining in account period steps from a maximum at the start of the contract to zero by the last accounting period. The depth of the steps of the theoretical basis (the fair-value premium) will be governed by interest rate changes and dividend adjustments.

Figure 3.4 shows this effect for the FT-SE March 1991 futures contract. For most of this quarter the futures contract was trading at a premium to its fair-value, and this is demonstrated by the jagged line of the simple basis; only briefly early in the quarter and close to the contract expiry do we see the simple basis line below the theoretical basis. As expected, this period of consistent high premium corresponds to an upward move in the equity market. Figure 3.5 gives us confirmation of this. As with Figure 3.4, the

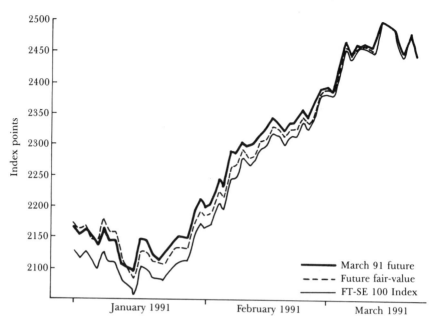

Figure 3.5　An upward move in the equity market

three lines will converge to a point for the expiry of the futures contract. On expiry the futures contract will be at its theoretical fair-value, which by definition will be the index level at that time.

We have looked at a period when the futures contract traded almost exclusively at a premium to its fair-value. Trading levels will, of course, oscillate either side of the theoretical fair level with a strong tendency to trade at much higher premiums whenever the market is perceived to be in a bullish mood, and below fair-value during bearish phases. Watching for these changes in the futures contracts can give significant information about the changing mood of a market before this becomes apparent in the underlying equity market. A futures contract that has been trading at a significant discount to its fair-value suddenly starting to show a premium, or a futures contract noticeably increasing its premium far above fair-value, should cause one to suspect that it might be wrong to be short of stock. Conversely, a sudden loss of premium on the futures contract should send some warning signals to all comitted bulls.

Some of the terms encountered in fair-value considerations include:

simple basis   = actual futures price—index level

theoretical basis or   = fair futures price—index level
fair-value premium

value basis   = actual futures price—fair futures price

Arbitrage between stocks and futures

Sometimes also known as programme trading, this activity seeks to generate profits whenever the futures contract is trading far out of line from its fair price. In simple terms, if the futures contract is trading expensively, i.e. above its fair-value, we can purchase the 100 equities in their correct weightings so as to duplicate the FT-SE 100 Index, and sell the expensively priced futures contracts against this. At expiry of the futures contract, which by definition will expire at the cash index level at that time, the equities are sold and a net arbitrage profit will result. There is, of course, no reason to run the arbitrage position to expiry of the futures contract other than to guarantee the arbitrage profit. Once the arbitrage position has been opened it may become viable to unwind it early because the futures contract has subsequently returned to trading at or even below its fair-value. Market makers or traders with the ability to 'lend' stock can also open arbitrage positions on the other side, i.e. short of stock and long of undervalued futures contracts. Figure 3.4, which gives the theoretical basis against the simple basis of the FT-SE 100 futures contract, shows that for this period only about two or three occasions were seen when the future was trading below its fair-value; for the rest of the time it was trading at a premium (not necessarily typical of the performance of other futures contracts). This does not, however, mean that for most of the period we should have been selling futures and buying equities, and all the rest of the time, early and late in the quarter, opening an opposite arbitrage or unwinding our position. In all the calculations so far we have used a mid-price for the index and the future, as well as for the costs of finance. We are all sadly aware that even if the price of stocks does not change, it costs more to buy than the indicated mid-price, and when we sell we get less than the indicated mid-price. Also, whenever we trade we incur dealing commissions both on equities and futures. These are the costs of the 'dealing-turn', and as the following shows, they are likely to be at least 1½ per cent.

Cost of arbitrage

	Stocks	Futures	Total
Bid/offer spread	1.0%	0.1%	1.1%
Commission	0.4%	0.05%	0.45%
			1.55%

Without the abolition of Stamp Duty in the UK, the cost of dealing (other than for market makers) is 0.5 per cent more expensive. So far, not all European countries have eliminated such or similar duties, and these must be included in costings where applicable.

As an arbitrageur is likely to want a profit of at least ½ per cent for his trouble, and 1 per cent if at all possible, we are looking for the futures contract to be trading 2 per cent out of line before serious arbitrage activity is likely to be seen. In other words, if the index stands at 2400 then the futures contract should be trading about 48 points above or below its fair-value for arbitrage to be attractive. The exact level may be slightly different for traders with differing costs and opportunities, such as trading inside the bid-offer spread.

Figure 3.6, a simplified view of how a stock index futures contract might behave, shows three occasions when the future was trading above the 'cost of arbitrage boundary' and three occasions when it fell below this band. These were the moments when an arbitrage window had opened and profitable arbitrage trades were, in theory at least, possible. For the rest of the time the futures contract was contained within the arbitrage band.

It is not unknown for a futures contract to break out of its arbitrage boundary and trade (on the upside) at considerable premiums, with no arbitrage activity to push it back into the 'cost of arbitrage boundary'. The explanation is that as arbitrageurs will in the main be the market makers themselves they will only arbitrage if they can show a net return on the operation. There is no point in making a £50 000 arbitrage profit only to lose £250 000 on the market-making book. Thus, although arbitrage in theory may be possible, in practice while there may be no difficulty in selling highly priced futures contracts, it may be impossible to buy the stock for the other side of the arbitrage. This fact in itself is useful information—the market is short of stock so the price will remain firm. By corollary we could expect that once arbitrage activity is seen to start (i.e. it is now possible to buy stock against

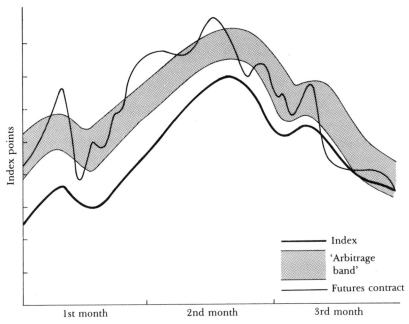

Figure 3.6   A simplified view of how a stock index futures might
behave

our short future position) then with stock becoming available the
market will be vulnerable to a fall in price.

Bull and bear fair-values

The usual fair-value figure that is quoted is that of a 'bull' fair-
value, where futures contracts are used as an alternative to stock
purchase. This fair-value is calculated on mid-prices of stocks, and
the cost of borrowing money based on a risk-free interest rate (like
UK Treasury Bills).

A 'bear' fair-value also exists, reflecting the lower interest earnt
on short futures positions and borrowing stock for delivery against
these short sales.

While a 'bear' fair-value may not be of direct interest to most
investors, it is important to an arbitrageur looking to open a short
stock long futures position. It will be a lower figure than the 'bull'
fair-value as it is calculated on an interest rate approximately 1
per cent lower than that used for the 'bull' fair-value, (the lending
rate as opposed to the borrowing rate).

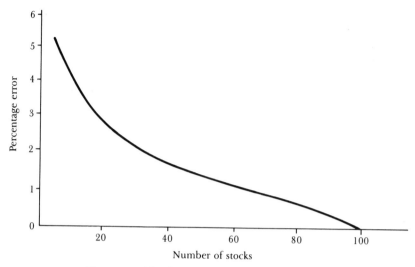

Figure 3.7 Tracking error for the FT-SE 100 Index

Arbitrage tracking error

While it may seem daunting to be dealing in 100 equities at the same time in order to execute an arbitrage order, in practice this is not so. As mentioned in our introduction, stock indices are products of the computer age. So too are arbitrage transactions. Automatic price data feeds to arbitrage programmes ensure almost instantaneous action by however many market-makers need to be involved. There is little to be gained by attempting to arbitrage between the futures contract and, say, 70 of the most highly weighted shares of the FT-SE 100 futures contract. The tracking error that we should have to consider has the following profile.

If we are aiming for a 1 per cent arbitrage profit but only using 70 equities then our 1 per cent arbitrage profit would carry a tracking error risk of almost 1 per cent. On unwinding our imperfect arbitrage we could find our expected profit to range between zero and double to that of a perfect (100 equity) arbitrage (Figure 3.7).

With the considerably fewer stocks employed in the CAC-40 and DAX indices, there is very little point in even considering anything other than a complete arbitrage of all the stocks in the index against its futures contract in the French and German as well as other European markets.

Fair-value when rolling from near to far futures contracts

In an earlier section we looked at how fair-value was calculated on a particular futures contract. Most futures contracts are for periods of three months or less. An investor with a horizon greater than the expiry of the current volume traded futures contract will have to close his current positions and open new ones in later contract months in order to maintain required market exposure. This process of 'rolling' contracts from a near to a far date can involve the investor or fund manager in considerable pricing risks, as well as providing price advantages and trading opportunities.

Just as the nearby futures contract has a calculated fair-value based on financing rates and best available dividend information, so too has the next futures contract. Assuming that we are considering a quarterly futures contract, like the FT-SE 100 future, and using, for simplicity, the simple formula for fair-value premium, then:

if: June is the current futures contract and still has one month to expiry,
interest rates are 11% pa
dividends are 4.5% pa
the index stands at 2550

$$\text{June F} = 2550 \times \left[\frac{(11 - 4.5)}{100} \times \frac{1}{12} \right] = 13.8$$

$$\text{September F} = 2550 \times \left[\frac{(11 - 4.5)}{100} \times \frac{4}{12} \right] = 55.3$$

The correct fair-value premium for the differential between June and September would therefore be 55.3 − 13.8 = 41.5 points. This differential will, of course, remain constant between the two contracts so long as interest rates and perceived dividends are unchanged. At expiry of the June contract, when June will have a fair value of zero, then the differential becomes the fair-value premium for the September contract in its own right.

Once we know the correct fair-value premium of the differential we know that at that level, 41.5 points in this instance, we can roll either our long or short positions from the nearby to the forward contract and suffer no financial penalty on the transaction (other than brokerage). However, as with straight trading of a particular contract month, so with the differential, there is every likelihood that market forces will pull the differential one way or another. If the differential between the two contract months reduces then the forward contract is trading cheap against fair-value. This is to the advantage of investors seeking to maintain a long futures position in the market. They simply sell their existing long futures position in the nearby contract and at the same time buy new futures contracts in the forward contract. The level at which the underlying index is trading is irrelevant. The order is given and transacted as a 'spread' order where only the spread, or differential between the two contracts is of import. Only once the spread order has been executed will the counterparties agree market levels for the outright months so as to be as far as possible in line with levels of straight trading in the separate contracts.

The further below the fair-value differential that the fund manager can roll his long positions, the greater the added value that he accrues to his fund, but the greater the pain suffered by the counterparty rolling a short position. And, similarly, should the market price of the differential increase to above its fair-value level, then rollers of long positions will be losing value while holders of short positions will be gaining. A curiously compensating factor here is that in a bull market holders of long positions will in any event be showing a profit on their positions. Consequently, the marginal adverse effect of having to pay a premium when rolling one's long position to the forward contract is rarely regarded as detrimental. Holders of short positions, on the other hand, although losing a capital sum may console themselves that their short hedge position (because that is what we hope it is—see Chapter 9 on hedging) is adding value to a market-direction-neutral fund! The opposite arguments can, of course, be used in a bear scenario.

Traders who believe that the differential will move in a particular direction can take appropriate action in order to profit from their view. Not infrequently do we see a spread quotation somewhat away from fair-value, and out of line with what is happening in the nearby futures contract. For instance, with one month before expiry the nearby contract may be trading at a substantial premium over its fair-value. The differential, on the other hand, may be indicated at somewhat below its fair-value owing to a temporary lack of buying interest on the forward future. It would, therefore, seem reasonable, so long as the market retains its generally bullish stance, that as the nearby contract gets closer to its expiry it will start to lose its excess premium, which will be transferred to the forward contract. We, therefore, sell the nearby future and buy the forward futures contract at an apparently low differential. Once our strategy is proved correct, we unwind the position by buying back our nearby short and selling out the forward long position at the higher differential. Our profit is assured no matter what has happened to the underlying market, as shown in the following example:

purchase September future @ 2655

sell   June   future @ 2614
_____

differential   41 points

Later we unwind this position when differential has increased and the market has also moved up sharply:

sell September future @ 3028

buy June   future @ 2969
_____

differential   59 points

profit on September position = 3028 − 2655 = 373 points

loss on June position   = 2614 − 2969 = 355 points

net profit on transaction   = 373 −   355 = 18 points

It is as well at this point to be aware of some rather confusing technicalities when placing spread orders. On the LIFFE an order to buy the nearby and sell the forward futures contract is abbreviated to 'buy the spread'. In order to unwind this position we 'sell the spread'. This leads to the oddity that in order to make a profit we have to buy at a high price and sell at a low price (for 'price' here of course think in terms of 'differential'). On the US markets an order to 'buy the spread' would mean to buy the forward future and sell the nearby, the complete opposite of the UK. It is as well, therefore, to double check with one's broker that in these transactions each party is fully aware just which contract has to be bought and which sold. Incidentally, a far less confusing nomenclature is used in the metal markets in London where spread orders are replaced by orders either to 'borrow' or 'lend'. If only these self-explanatory terms could be used in stock index contracts!

Table 3.1   Various stock index futures contract sizes.

Contract	Index level	Multiplier	Contract value
FT-SE 100	2450	£25	£61 250
DAX–30	1625	DM100	DM162 500
CAC-40	1850	FF200	FF370 000
EOE	327	Dfl200	Dfl65 400
S & P 500	328	US$500	US$189 000
Nikkei 225	26275	Y1000	Y26 275 000

Quoted index levels are for illustration only (but were seen in the early half of 1991). Therefore, if we purchase eight CAC-40 futures contracts at an index level of 1850, and later sell them at an index level of 1892, our profit will be:

$$(1892 - 1850) \times FF\ 200 \times 8 = FF\ 67\ 200$$

Alternatively, if we sold 35 FT-SE 100 Index futures contracts at an index level of 2555, but closed our position when the index had risen to 2610, we would realize a loss of:

$$(2555 - 2610) \times £25 \times 35 = (£48\ 125)$$

Futures contract size

The futures contract size, or underlying equity equivalent value, is the index level multiplied by a defined factor. In the UK this multiplier is £25, so for a futures level of 2450 the contract size will be $2450 \times £25 = £61\ 250$. An investor wishing to open a £10 000 000 exposure to the equity market via the FT-SE 100 futures contract would therefore buy (at a futures level of 2450):

$$\frac{10\ 000\ 000}{61250} = 163 \text{ futures contracts}$$

Table 3.1 shows the contract sizes for European stock index futures contracts as well as some US and Japanese contracts by way of comparison.

Margin trading

When opening a futures position, the investor does not, of course, pay out the underlying equity equivalant value (£61 250 in the previous example). He only puts up a small percentage of the contract value as margin. A margin is a good faith deposit made by a client to a broker in order to maintain a futures or options contract. The minimum amount that is required will be set by the exchange where the contract is traded. Currently on the FT-SE

100 Index this amount is £2500 per contract so with the index at 2450, and one contract therefore representing an equity equivalent value of £61 250, this margin accounts for only some 4 per cent of total exposure. Should market volatility suddenly increase, the governing exchange may well decide to increase margin requirements. Normally, futures market margins are of the order of 4 or 5 per cent of the underlying contract value, and the broker will ask his commercial clients for the same margin.

For private clients a broker may well ask for double margin in order to provide additional security on what is after all a highly geared investment. Should the market move up 4 per cent once our investor has opened his long futures position (and 4 per cent is only 98 points on an index standing at 2450, not impossible on a very good day, and certainly possible on a fair three-day bull run), our investor, who tends only to look at his margin and not the underlying value, will consider that he has done extremely well in that he has doubled his money. On the other hand, a fall in the market of 6 per cent overnight (modest compared to living memory) would wipe out the investor's entire deposited margin and leave him owing his broker a further 50 per cent of his initial investment—not a happy set of circumstances. Gearing is certainly a two-edged sword. Higher gearing means increased risk and higher potential profits. The much higher margins that exchange regulatory authorities may set at times of high volatility, effectively discourage trading because the considerably reduced gearing is no longer attractive to many futures traders.

It is this gearing effect that causes many problems with the uninitiated and leads the gentlemen of the popular press to describe futures trading as little better than wild gambling. This is unjustified, but there is a strong case to be made for educating all investors on the dangers of dealing in an instrument that magnifies the movement of the underlying market 25 fold.

Margining example

A client buys 50 futures contracts at 2455 to open a position and deposits £300 000 margin with his broker. At the end of the first day the future closes at 2440. The client's account looks like this:

margin deposited	300 000
initial margin on 50 contracts	(125 000)
surplus on initial margin	175 000

adjustment for variation in price
$$- 15 \times 50 \times 25 \qquad \underline{(18\ 750)}$$

surplus at end of first day   156 250

During the second day the market rises and the client closes his position at 2465. The account now looks as follows:

surplus carried over   156 250

adjustment for variation
in price 25 × 50 × 25   31 250

returned initial margin   <u>125 000</u>

account balance   312 500

The benefit of depositing a sum in excess of the initial margin is shown in this example when the price moves adversely on the first day. If only the £125 000 had been deposited there would have been a requirement for further margin or maintanance margin; however, the excess in the account eliminated this need. Such surplus funds are normally paid interest at overnight deposit rates, subject to agreed minimum deposits.

To summarize, there are three major benefits of dealing on a margin:

1. Profits and losses are clearly shown each day.
2. Substantial gearing is available.
3. The clearing house can provide insurance against default.
   More on this in a later chapter.

Dealing costs compared for equities options and futures

We need to make the following assumptions in order to make accurate comparisons of dealing costs:

1. The FT-SE 100 Index stands at 2420 in January. The March Stock Exchange Index 2400 puts are 50p.
2. The investor has a £5 million portfolio that tracks the index exactly. For a portfolio of this size, the equivalent numbers of futures contracts would be:

$$\frac{5\ 000\ 000}{2420 \times 25} = 83 \text{ to the nearest whole contract}$$

The number of options contracts required to replicate the portfolio would be:

$$\frac{5\ 000\ 000}{2400 \times 10} = 208$$

3. Commissions in the three markets are as follows—LIFFE: £20 per contract for a 'round trip' (buying or selling to open a position as well as the subsequent closing transaction). The Stock Exchange (ISE): 0.2 per cent each way. The London Traded Options Market (LTOM): 501 per contract plus 1 per cent of the options consideration each way (Table 3.2).

4. Typical bid/offer dealing spreads in the three markets are as follows:

   LIFFE: two index points at £25 per point

   ISE: 1 per cent of the portfolio value

   LTOM: five points at £10 per point

5. Assume no other regulatory charges such as Stamp Duty or Taxes.

Table 3.2   Comparative costs of trading a portfolio value of £ 5 million by futures, options and equities

	LIFFE	LTOM		ISE	
Commission	83 × 20 = 1660	208 + (208 × 0.5 × 1000 × 1%)	= 1248	5m × 0.4% = 20 000	
Dealing spread	83 × 50 = 4150	208 × 5 × 10	= 10 400	5m × 1%	= 50 000
Total	£5810		£11 648		£70 000
% of £ 5m	0.12%		0.23%		1.40%

The cost of trading equities rather than futures is almost 12 times as high, and the procedures are considerably more cumbersome. Trading in options is roughly twice as expensive as trading in futures.

CHAPTER 4

Index options and warrants

A traded option gives the buyer of the option the right, but not the obligation to buy or sell the instrument to which the option relates, at a fixed price on or before a fixed date in the future. In the case of index options, the buyer, or holder of the option, has the right to buy or sell a nominal amount of the underlying index, at a predetermined index level, at any time up to the expiry of the option.

Considerable strategic complexity can be developed using a combination of options, or options and futures. There are, however, only two types of option, a call option and a put option.

1. *Call option*   This will allow the buyer of the call option to buy the index at a fixed level during the life of the option.

2. *Put option*   This will allow the buyer of the put to sell the index at a fixed level during the life of the option.

The buyer's risk is, therefore, limited to the premium that he pays. If the market fails to perform in the expected manner, and the option buyer does not cut his loss, he will in time lose the entire premium paid (except in the case of in-the-money options). The option seller's (or writer's) risk is unlimited as he may be obliged to sell or buy the index at seriously disadvantageous levels in order to meet contractual obligations. Option writers, for this reason, have to comply with very strict exchange rules of financial standing and collateral, and therefore tend to be market professionals.

Table 4.1 Example of option prices in the CAC-40 Index at 1760 (in early August)

Strike prices		Call prices	Put prices
September	1675	110	3.40
	1700	80	5.50
	1725	60	9.25
	1750	38	16
	1775	22	25
	1800	12	42

Above the double line calls are in-the-money; below this puts are in-the-money.

Strike prices and expiry

Traded options allow the holder to buy or sell stock at a predetermined price. This price is known as the 'strike price' or 'exercise price' of the option. The levels at which strike prices are set are predetermined by the governing exchange and will be either side of the underlying market level. As the market moves away from the median, new higher or lower levels will be introduced. An example of option prices on the CAC-40 is given in Table 4.1.

Traded options all have a limited lifespan, ceasing on their expiry date. The actual date in the month at which an option expires will vary from exchange to exchange. In London, the index options expire at 11.20 of the last trading day in the month; on several other European exchanges, it is the third Wednesday of the contract month. Full details are given in Appendix 2 on stock index contract details. Usually the longest dated index options that can be traded expire 12 months ahead, but most trading volume is seen in the nearest three months. A particular advantage of index options over futures can be the fact that whereas futures contracts tend to be quarterly, usually following the March, June, September and December cycle, traded options contracts are available for the nearest three consecutive months.

Premium and margin

For every option buyer, there must be a willing seller. The price at which the seller is offering calls and puts will be displayed either on a 'Public Limit Order Board' or electronically, as are the bids from the buyers. These are the 'prices' or 'premiums' that the buyer pays the seller for an option. Whenever a bargain is traded it is important that the client advises the broker whether the deal is an opening trade or closing trade. This information is necessary as it is used to cancel liabilities. Any sold option is, in isolation, a liability and so whenever a closing purchase is made it is vital that the market is aware that the original liability has been cancelled. This information also allows an accurate record to be kept in the market of the degree of 'open interest' in each contract.

As 'short' option positions are liabilities, holders of short options positions have to put up a margin in much the same way as in the futures market. The degree of margin required (different for different exchanges) basically has to reflect the degree of risk that the writer has entered into. On the LTOM the total margin requirement at any one time is 12½ per cent of the value plus or minus the amount that the option is in-the-money or out-of-the-money. When combinations of options reduce risk, as in bull spreads, a lower margin requirement is applied. Enlightened exchanges will also allow reduced margin requirements if option risk is offset by a compatible stock index futures position. Although cash can be used for margin requirements, in the options market in particular it is more usual to use some other instrument as collateral, such as Treasury Bills, Certificates of Deposit, etc.

Example

Margin requirement on the London Traded Options Market for writer of a call option.

index stands at 2602 in August

September 2550 call quoted 105–108

for one call written at 105

$$\text{margin} = 12\tfrac{1}{2}\% \times 2602 = 325.25$$
$$2602 - 2550 = \underline{52}$$
$$377.25$$

$377.25 \times £10$ (contract size) $= £3772.50$

As the option writer receives a premium of $105 \times £10 = £1050$, actual cash requirement is $£3772.50 - £1050 = £2722.50$ per contract. Commission has been omitted from the calculation.

Exercise and assignment

If the holder of an option wishes to take up the right to buy or sell the underlying index, he or she will 'exercise' the option. Almost all options now traded are of the 'American' variety, which allow the holder to exercise before expiry if the investor feels that this is advantageous. By contrast, the traditional or so called 'European' options (not quite as popular, even in Europe) are only allowed to be exercised on expiry day.

Once an investor exercises the option, via a broker, the clearing house will issue an 'assignment notice' to a broker, picked by a computerized random selection process, requesting that its client, the option writer, fulfils the terms of the option contract.

The whole process of 'exercise' is, however, more suited to options on equities where an exercise stock is either called for or is delivered; index options can either be cash settled, in which case they are closed at the prevailing market price, or they may have as their underlying instrument a futures contract on the same index. Under these circumstances, exercise will result in a long or short futures position which can either be retained or traded out in the futures market. More usually, index options positions will, however, be closed out in the normal course of trading, rather than via the exercise route.

Factors influencing options prices

The price or level of the underlying index will be the main influence on an index options value. A call will thus become more valuable as the underlying index rises while a put will become more valuable as the index falls. A stock index call can also be considered as an alternative to possessing stock, and a holder of calls makes an opportunity gain by not having to pay finance charges on holding the underlying stock. High interest rates can, therefore, be seen to increase call premiums. Puts are an alternative to shorting stock and are thus less valuable with high financing charges as interest could be gained on the short stock position.

With other considerations equal, an option with a long life will be more valuable than one that is going to expire shortly, simply because it will have more chance of being in-the-money at some time during its life.

Deep in-the-money options will also have a built-in value that increases the deeper in-the-money they go. At-the-money options can almost be regarded as futures contracts that will make a profit (less premium) in one direction, and only lose the options premium in the other direction. We can thus summarize the option price influencing factors considered so far as:

- The price of the underlying asset or index level
- Financing costs
- The length of time before expiry of the option
- The degree to which an option is in-the-money or out-of-the-money.

A final factor to consider in option pricing is volatility, an area that deserves a section to itself.

Volatility

This is defined as 'the degree to which the price of a stock, commodity or cash index tends to fluctuate over a defined period of time'. In order to understand it more fully it is as well to break volatility down into three distinctive categories.

1. Historical volatility

This refers to the range of price movements that have been seen in a particular stock or index over a specified time in the past. Using price data for the period of time under consideration, the volatility, or to give it its proper statistical term, 'standard deviation', can be calculated using the formula given below. From these calculations a figure is obtained for the standard deviation over a defined period, like the last month or the last year. Depending on which period is used, the volatility may vary considerably so, in order to be of use, obviously like must be compared with like.

Looking at some actual numbers, the annualized volatility for the FT-SE 100 Index for the period shown in Figure 4.1 gives an average of about 14 per cent and has ranged between 11½ per cent and 15½ per cent. In crude terms the index is demonstrating

Figure 4.1 One-year historic FT-SE 100 volatility

an average 14 per cent move per annum. The volatility of the CAC-40 is shown for comparison in Figure 4.2.

Monthly volatilities may, of course, be higher and weekly volatilities higher still. Extremes of movement like the crash of October 1987 last only for a few days. The shorter the period that we are considering, the higher the volatility is likely to be.

The statistical correlation between volatility and time is governed by the square root of time:

annualized volatility = monthly volatility $\times \sqrt{12}$

and

annualized volatility = weekly volatility $\times \sqrt{52}$

Thus an annualized volatility represents a monthly volatility of about 4 per cent or a weekly volatility of about 1.9 per cent.

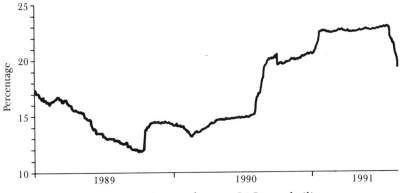

Figure 4.2 One-year historic CAC-40 volatility

For the actual calculation of volatility we use the following formula:

$$\sqrt{\sum_{i=1}^{N}\left(\frac{(R_i - R)^2}{N-1}\right)}$$

where R_i = observations i on variable R
$\quad\quad$ R = the average of Ri
$\quad\quad$ i = 1, 2, 3 . . . N
$\quad\quad$ N = number of observations in sample

From a database of prices we can, therefore, calculate volatilities for any period. The historical data is then used to compare with what is happening this week or this month. Specifically when using the options market we would be looking for prices that exhibit anomalously high or low levels of volatility compared to historical data and trade from the standpoint that over time the anomalous volatilities will drift back towards the norm.

2. Implied volatility

In the option markets, volatility considerations are paramount since volatility is one of the key determinants of an option price. The theoretical value of an option is calculated using a pricing model in which time, interest rates, volatility and the intrinsic value of the option are input, in order to produce the option premium quoted in the market.

It is, therefore, possible by changing the equation of the calculation to determine the volatility implicit in any price at which an option might be trading. Implied volatility can, therefore, be defined as the volatility implied by the current option price. UK stock index options tend to show an average annualized volatility of about 23 per cent while stock options themselves show a higher figure, about 30 per cent. Within these general indications will be companies whose shares exhibit minimal movement, like TSB whose options trade on volatilities of only 26 per cent. At the other end of the scale are companies like Amstrad and Consolidated Goldfields which regularly show annualized volatilities of 34 or 35 per cent per annum.

3. Projected volatility

This is simply an estimate of future volatility based on historical volatility, market analysis and the personal view of the investor. All options trading is to some degree taking a view on projected volatility as not only do we hope that we have backed a correct market view, but also that it is the correct view within a defined time frame, like the life of the option.

The greater the volatility of the index the greater must be the price of the option. Clearly, there is more chance of making a substantial profit out of the option if the underlying market is undergoing violent movement. We can, therefore, start to develop strategies that will gain or lose according to the volatility of the market. In general, the trader buying volatility will profit if the market then moves with increased uncertainty thereby causing option premiums to rise; the volatility seller, meanwhile, hopes for a quiet, inactive period on the market. As a result, we could expect the volatility seller to make modest profits most of the time, but suffer the occasional large loss and the volatility buyer to take several small losses and the occasional large profit.

In the short term, the price of an option is governed exclusively by volatility. In order to be able to speculate on volatility predictions and their associated price changes, it is important to understand how the sensitivity of an options premium changes relative to the variables that affect pricing. This measurement of sensitivity is known as delta and is defined below.

Delta

The amount by which an option's price should change for a corresponding change in the price of the underlying index (or equity). Call options deep in-the-money will have delta close to 1, and will, therefore, move closely in line with the index. Deep in-the-money puts will show delta close to -1. Far out-of-the money options have delta values close to zero and thus show little response in changes to the underlying index.

A delta of 0.5, therefore, means that for a one-point index move, the option will move 0.5 points.

As an option moves from being out-of-the money to in-the-money so the delta increases, the increase being greatest for shorter

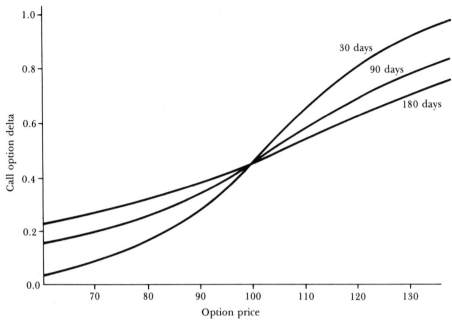

Figure 4.3 Premium convexity: change of delta against price

dated options. This manifests itself as a premium gain on the option as shown in Figure 4.3.

The other measures of sensitivity that are used in option pricing models are given below.

Gamma

This is the amount by which an options delta will move after a one-point move in the level of the underlying index (Figure 4.4). It is the proportional change in delta for a given change in the index level. A gamma of 0.1 will thus move the delta from 0.5 to 0.6 for a one-point move in the underlying index. Gamma will be greatest for at-the-money options close to expiry.

Rho

This quantifies the effect on the value of an option of a 1 per cent change in financing costs, i.e. it is interest rate sensitive.

Theta

Theta represents the daily price decay that affects an option as it ages and loses time value (Figure 4.5). Thus, if the underlying

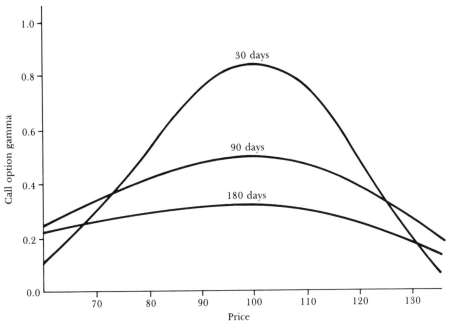

Figure 4.4 Change of gamma against price

index remains constant, a theta of 0.02 will cause a daily decay in the option value of 0.02. As with gamma, theta exhibits greatest effect close to the expiry of the option.

Kappa
(also known as vega) This represents the change in the value of an option due to a 1 per cent change in volatility. Thus if the volatility of the index increases from 14 per cent to 16 per cent, a kappa of 0.2 would imply a premium increase of 0.4 per cent.

The pricing of options

Having considered the many factors affecting the value of options, we can now turn to the subject of the pricing of options. Most investors will have little need in understanding the mathematics behind options calculations (which are also used to evaluate warrant prices). It is, however, as well to be aware of some of the considerations employed in the more popular pricing models. This correctly suggests that there is no universally accepted method of

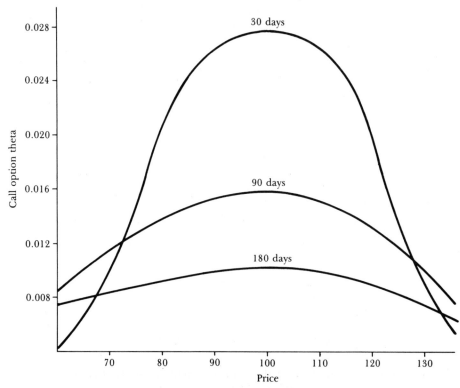

Figure 4.5 Change of theta with price

options pricing. In fact, several mathematical models exist, which in turn have spawned many clones and adaptations. The more the pure mathematician strives for perfection, the more complex and cumbersome do the considerations become, with little or no gain in helping one to become a more efficient trader. Two pricing models of which the investor should, however, be aware of are the 'Black & Scholes' and the binomial model.

The Black & Scholes Model

This was originally published in 1973, and for ease of computation made certain assumptions:

1. The option is a European-style option, thus there are no early exercise possibilities.
2. There are no dealing costs or taxes.

3. The risk-free interest rate (i.e. for instruments such as gilts) is known and is constant throughout the life of the option.
4. The volatility of the underlying instrument (or index) is known and remains constant over the life of the option.
5. The distribution of possible share prices or index levels at the end of a period of time is lognormal in nature. This essentially means that the share or index being considered is as likely to double in value as it is to halve (or go up in value as to go down). It also implies that share prices or indices cannot become negative.

With these provisions in mind, the B & S model provides the following formula for the value of a call option:

$$\text{value of call option} = SN(d_1) - Ee^{-rT} N(d_2)$$

$$\text{where } d_1 = \frac{\log (S/E) + rT + V^2T/2}{V(NT)}$$

$$d_2 = d_1 - V(NT)$$

S = share price
E = exercise price
T = time to expiry in years
r = risk-free interest rate continuously compounded
log = natural logarithm function
V = annualized volatility of the index
N = cumulative normal distribution function

The formula is complex, but in essence it is made up of the three factors that affect the value of options, namely, the degree to which an option is in or out-of-the-money, the risk-free interest rate to the time of expiry and the historical volatility.

Although one of the early assumptions for the B & S formula was that there would be no early exercise of the option, the model can be amended to give some allowance for American-style options. This can be done by regarding each American-style option as an integral part of a series of compounded European-style options, and making the necessary adjustments to the calculations.

The binomial model

While the B & S calculations of options prices are based on straightforward mathematical assumptions, the binomial model uses a numerical approach. It assumes that if one observes a share price at the start and the end of a period of time (a binomial step) the share price will take one of two known values at the end of that period. The share price will move either up or down by a predetermined amount. As the number of time periods increase, the probability distribution approaches the normal distribution, or common 'bell shaped' curve. Because of this step-by-step approach, the model can accommodate specific events such as dividends or conversions during the life of a put or call option. In other words, the binomial model arives at the value of an option by taking the present value of the various possible expiration values of the option multiplied by the probabilities that those values will occur. Mathematically, this can be represented as follows: if P is the price, and the rate of return on the share after an incremental period of time is either

U with a probability of q

or D with a probability of (1-q)

then after one time period the price will have one of the following two values:

UP with a probability of q

or DP with a probability of (1-q)

The expected return after this one time period is therefore:

q (UP + (1-q) (DP)

If r = (1 + riskless rate) then the above should equall rP. Therefore:

$$q(UP) + (1-q)(DP) = rP$$

$$\text{probability } q = \frac{r - D}{U - D}$$

Using a tree diagram, we can represent the above time periods, extended to a very large number of steps:

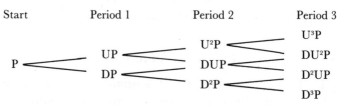

Figure 4.6   Tree diagram representing certain time periods

For instance, at Period 3 for the top and bottom nodes, U^3P and D^3P, there is only one possible route by which the price can be obtained from the start. U^3P would have to have moved up all the way, D^3P, down. For the intervening nodes, DU^2P and D^2UP, there are three routes by which the final price can be obtained, thus the probability of arriving at each of the four final nodes is 1:3:3:1.

Once the 'tree' pattern has been constructed, and knowing the possible values of the option at expiry, the values at the tips of the branches of the tree, it is a relatively easy matter to work out fair-values for the option at all the earlier nodes and so get a theoretical fair value for any point on the price tree. This is done by comparing the value of holding and the value of prompt exercise at each node along the price tree and choosing the optimum value. The process is then repeated at each node, back to the base of the tree. An advantage of this method is that not only do we obtain the fair price at any point but also the optimum exercise point.

Binomial pricing example
Let us assume that an index stands at 2600 and will move, with equal probability, by either +10 or −5 at each step. In three steps the option will expire and we now wish to determine the fair price of an American exercise put option at 2605.

The price tree shows price movements over time with four possible terminal branches at 2630, 2615, 2600 and 2585:

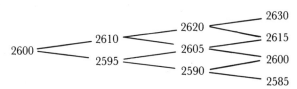

Figure 4.7 A price tree showing price movements over time with four possible terminal branches

One step before expiry, with the index at 2620, 2605 or 2590, our option will have the following values:

1. If the market is at 2620, the next step will result in our put option at 2605 expiring worthless, therefore at 2620 the option already has a value of zero.
2. At 2605 our option has an even chance of expiring worthless,

and an even chance of expiring worth 5. As immediate exercise is not worth while because the option is out-of-the-money, the present value of the option must be 2.5.

3. At the 2590 node, the option, with one step to expiry, has a value of: $(0.5 - 5) + (0.5 \times 20) = 12.5$. Prompt exercise of the option would, however, give us $2605 - 2590 = 15$. As this is preferable, this is the correct valuation and the option should be exercised.

Using the same logic we can determine the values of the option at nodes where the index is 2610 and 2595, two steps before expiry. This will give us a value of $0.5 \times (0 + 2.5) = 1.25$ at 2610 and an immediately exercisable value of 10 at 2595. The process can now be completed a final time to give a value of $0.5 \times (1.25 + 10) = 5.625$ at the base of the tree. As at this point prompt exercise would only give a value of 5.0, then 5.625 is the correct value.

Although this step-by-step approach is fairly straightforward once the principle is grasped, it does suffer from the fact that for most situations the high number of different possible routes that we have to consider will mean that the tree will have, possibly, 200 steps and 15 000 nodes. It is little wonder that with the complexity of the Black & Scholes calculation and the sheer volume of calculation required in the binomial model, that all options evaluation calculations now tend to be obtained from various computer models.

These two approaches to the valuation of options should in no way be regarded as the complete answer, but they do demonstrate the two major techniques employed. Other researchers have developed similar formulae for options valuation, just as the binominal model can also be refined and adapted to allow for increasingly complex considerations.

Binomial valuation of European-style option

One advantage that the binomial method has is that it can immediately cost a European-style option. As early exercise is not possible at each node we simply take the lowest value.

If we rework the option tree using the same index levels and step sizes, our European-style 2605 put will show the following values:

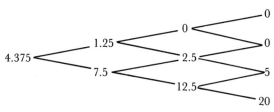

Figure 4.8 A reworked option tree

The put is, therefore, worth 4.375, cheaper by 1.25 than the American-style option. This differential between the two option styles represents the extra cost of the early exercise facility.

Differences between European and American options

Although American exercise options are generally more popular than the European-style options, there are several reasons why both have a place in the market place. European-style options, which can by definition only be exercised on expiry-day, at the same time give the option writer the assurance that there is no risk of early assignment. This can be a considerable advantage for fund managers who wish to construct portfolio strategies that could otherwise be negated by short or long positions suddenly arising from unexpected early exercise.

European-style options will always have lower premiums than American-style options because they offer less risk to the option writer. The actual price differential between the two option styles represents the risk that the writer carries in not being able to determine at which points the option may be exercised as a result of prompt value being higher than value at expiration. This differential has just been demonstrated using the binomial method of options valuation.

For investors who have no interest in early exercise, the cheapness of European-style options can be a significant attraction. Long-dated European-style options will also trade at a discount to the shorter ones, so price attraction will be even more significant the longer the period to exercise.

Uses of options

As with futures, options can be used both to speculate and to manage risk. The active trader is more likely to use index options for the former, the fund manager for the latter. Traded options have the flexibility to be used for many different strategies that are impossible with futures. Futures give only two alternatives, buying or selling, in which case one might argue that when trading futures the position will be either right or wrong. Options allow the trader to fine-tune risk exposure through selecting different exercise prices over selected periods of time. In-the-money options will have many of the characteristics of a futures position and while deep in-the-money options will carry high premiums they can be used to provide protection against an adverse price move. A cheaper out-of-the-money option will provide only limited protection against adverse price movement, reflecting the 'opportunity cost' nature of all options transactions.

Selecting the right options

Before considering the various strategies that one can employ using options, it is as well to be aware of how the effect of 'gearing' will translate itself into differing returns for different options series. Investors looking at option series for the first time are often bewildered by the seemingly vast choice of options available. It soon becomes apparent that one simply does not just buy a call because the market will move up. One has to be selective on the degree of risk-return that one is prepared to accept. Getting the right 'feel' for which option one should be trading under specific circumstances is really common sense, based on a bit of knowledge and tempered by one's own views.

Example

Using some actual figures for the UK market for 1989 we can see what happens to option prices at times of increased market movement. On 5 October and with the FT-SE 100 Index trading at 2310 the following option prices were quoted:

		Calls	Puts
October	2200	122–127	10–11
	2250	80–83	20–22
	2300	43–48	35–38
	2350	21–24	63–67
	2400	7–10	98–103

November	2250	106–111	32–35
	2300	73–78	49–53
	2350	45–48	75–78
	2400	26–29	107–112
	2450	13–16	135–140
December	2250	128–132	42–45
	2300	93–98	60–63
	2350	65–70	85–90
	2400	45–48	115–120
	2450	26–30	155–160

With the index at 2310, we decide that we are bullish of the market and expect it to rise quite soon. We can buy an at-the-money 2300 call option for October expiry at 48p, equivalent to £480 per contract on the London Traded Options Market. For us to show a profit the market does now need to go up quickly, and if we expect to run the position to the October expiry we need to see the contract close above 2348 (plus dealing costs) in order to make a profit.

If we are convinced that the market will rise, but not much before November, the November 2300 call would cost 78p, the extra 30p being the premium that we pay for the longer time that the option has to run. In this case, a position run to the end of November would break even at 2378. The December 2300 call is more expensive still.

If we strongly believed that the market was going to rise at least 50 points before the end of the month, the 2350 October call would have only cost 24p, but the break-even at the end of October is 2350 + 24 = 2374.

Had we been particularly astute we might have just decided that all this bullish sentiment was rather misplaced and the October 2250 puts at 22p were an interesting little investment. The end October break-even for these would be 2250 − 22 = 2228.

The following day, 6 October, saw a bit of a sell-off, and at one point the index stood at 2263. Prices for the October and December options were then quoted as follows:

		Calls	Puts
October	2250	47–52	31–33
	2300	23–27	56–60
	2350	8–9	85–90

December	2250	97–108	56–60
	2300	70–73	80–85
	2350	40–43	113–116

Our last minute impulse buy, the October 2250 puts could now be sold for 31p, showing us a 41 per cent profit overnight! Had we decided to trade at-the-money and purchased the 2300 puts for 38p, we could now sell these for 56p, an overnight return of 47 per cent. Looking at the December puts, because of the considerable time element they were only showing a profit of the order of 25 per cent—still not bad.

Call buyers unfortunately fared rather badly. The 2300 October calls lost over half their value while the 2350 calls over two thirds of their value. December 2300 calls fared a little better losing only about one third of their value.

Ten days later the market attempted a minor copy of the-great-crash-of-1987 and at one point on 16 October the index was trading at 2100. The October and December options then had the following values.

		Calls	Puts
October	2200	17–25	125–140
	2250	5–10	170–180
	2300	3–5	210–230
	2350	1–4	260–280
	2400	0–2	310–330
December	2250	50–70	200–225
	2300	20–30	240–260
	2350	13–23	280–300

Our great friend, the 2250 October put now had a sale value of 170p, a return of 673 per cent while the 2300 put with a value of 210p was showing by comparison a miserable 453 per cent profit (in 11 days). The 2300 put showed a greater return for the earlier smaller move, but was overtaken by the return on the 2250 put once that started to become closer to 'at-the-money'.

For comparison, the percentage profits or losses are shown here for purchases based on 5 October prices and sales on the 16 October prices.

		Calls	Puts
October	2200	−87%	+987%
	2250	−94%	+673%
	2300	−94%	+453%

December	2250	−62%	+344%
	2300	−80%	+281%
	2350	−81%	+211%

While opportunities such as provided by this example are not very common, the information that we can learn from it can be applied to all options trading. Firstly, the trader's ideal is to buy an out-of-the-money call or put, as nearby as possible, i.e. the nearest traded month, and then, happily, to discover that the market has moved such as to bring the option into-the-money in just a few days. Or, as in the case of the 2200 October put, to generate a 987 per cent return in 11 days!

If only things were so simple. The further out-of-the-money and the nearer the expiry, the cheaper the option. The risk to the option granter is less. A nearby option, far out-of-the-money, will erode in value faster than any other if the market fails to move, or the investor gets the direction wrong—after all, the 2400 October call dropped to zero in the same 11 days. Even if the investor gets the direction right, a slow moving market may erode time value at such a rate as to never let a deeply out-of-the money option show a profit. Deeply out-of-the-money nearby options should be considered as a low-cost but high-risk trade.

The closer that we trade to at-the-money, the less our potential gearing, but the more time we have before deciding whether to run a speculative position, if profitable, or cut if wrong. For a long-dated option, with say three months to expiry, we are paying a considerable portion for the time value. Other than getting a market view wrong, nothing is worse than buying a long-dated option and then watching it lose its value as a result of the non-movement of the market. It is all too easy to purchase such an option on the grounds that the market will move in a known direction at some time, but no one is sure just when. This really is tantamount to some rather poor armchair-trading. A far better case can be made for trading nearer dated options slightly out-of-the-money. If one's timing is less than perfect then the potential loss is not as great and the position can be closed. If necessary, a new position can then be opened in the next month. Shorter dated options force a healthier degree of discipline on the trader than do long-dated ones.

A final aspect of the example that we should consider is that of seeking to profit by a move in either direction. If on 5 October we had very strong feelings that the market was about to make a dramatic move, but really had no idea in which direction, we could have opened a double option—more commonly known as a long straddle. (The main options strategies will be covered in the following section.) With the market at 2310 and not certain of the direction of any coming large move, we purchase October 2350 calls at 24p and 2250 puts at 22p. Our total cost now is 46p (plus dealing costs), and the market by option expiry has to move above $2350 + 46 = 2396$ or below $2250 - 46 = 2204$ for our position to break even.

On the 16 October we could have unwound our position: 2350 calls sold at 1p, 2250 puts sold at 170p. Gain is therefore $171 - 46 = 125p$. Not as great a profit as demonstrated earlier, but similar to what we could have expected if the market had gone up 200 points instead. A danger of a long straddle, though, is that if the market fails to make a large move, time value will erode our options from both sides.

Options trading strategies

Options can be used on their own, in conjunction with the futures contract, or in a strategy using the underlying cash instrument (although as we are only considering stock indices, our underlying cash instrument is the represented equity market). Strategies can broadly be divided into three categories, directional trades, precision trades and locked trades.

1. Directional trades

Directional trades are used where the investor is looking for a particular direction to the market, and are used by both traders and hedges in a similar manner to futures. The major directional strategies are:

- long or short call
- long or short put
- bull spread
- bear spread.

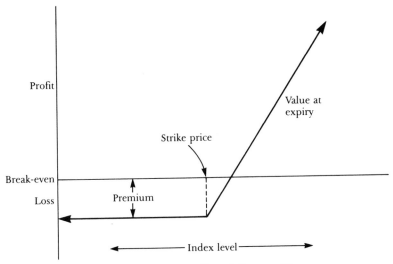

Figure 4.9 Long call profit/loss profile

Profit profiles on calls and puts

A long call, i.e. the purchase of a call, should be used when one expects that the market will rise. As seen in the earlier example, the more bullish one is of the market, the more out-of-the money the option that one should buy. For the option purchaser in this simple strategy loss is limited to the option premium while profit is potentially unlimited. The profit profiles are shown in Figures 4.9 and 4.10.

Profit increases as the market rises. The position is, however, a wasting asset because as time passes the value of the option erodes. The writer of the call will have a mirror image position along the break-even line. His profit will be limited to the premium received, but the potential loss should the market rise will be unlimited. Because of this open-ended risk such positions have to be closely monitored. A short call, however, is an appreciating asset—as time passes the value of the short call increases as the option loses time value.

A long put will gain value as the market comes down, and can thus be used either as a speculative bear play on the market, or as a hedge of an index-related equity fund. Again, loss is limited to the amount paid for the option and the maximum loss will be seen if the market ends above the option exercise level. As with the long call, the position is a wasting asset. If volatility in the market

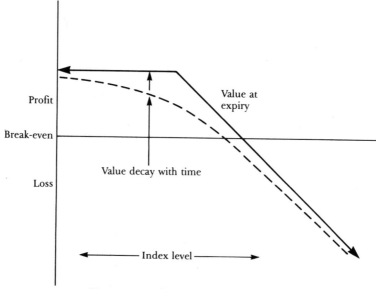

Figure 4.10   Short call profit/loss profile

increases the erosion of value slows; as volatility decreases the erosion of value speeds up (Figure 4.11).

Selling a put will give the seller a maximum profit of the

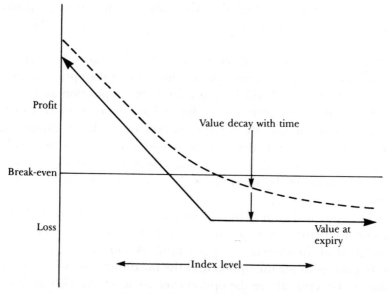

Figure 4.11   Long put profit/loss profile

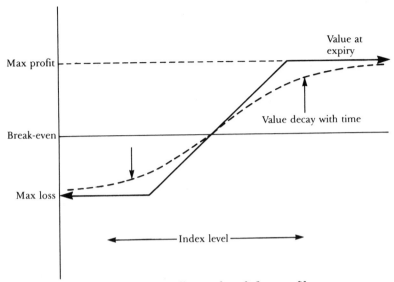

Figure 4.12 Bull spread profit/loss profile

premium received, but a potential unlimited loss should the market collapse. The profit loss profile would be a mirror image of that of the long put.

The selling of options, while risky, is a legitimate means of generating premium income, particularly if compensating market positions are held, such as a long futures or stock position against which calls can be written. Where an investor is particularly certain of, say, a coming bullish market move, he can write puts and use the premium generated to buy calls (the Texas hedge). Such strategies are, however, highly speculative.

Bull and bear spreads These are some of the most popular option strategies, in that they reflect the bullish or bearish sentiment of the trader, but not to any overwhelming degree. A bull spread is a good position to open if we want to be in the market but are unsure of expectations (Figure 4.12). We purchase a call and sell another call with the same expiry but a higher strike price. At expiry, if the stock remains below the lower strike price, both calls will expire worthless. The loss will, therefore, be limited to the initial cost of the spread. With the stock between the strike prices of the two calls, the purchased call is in-the-money while the sold call expires worthless. The overall profit is, therefore, the intrinsic value of the bought call less the initial debit. If the stock exceeds the higher of the strike prices, the maximum level of profit is reached, equal to the difference between the strike prices, less the initial debit.

A bull spread can also be created using puts. One put is purchased and simultaneously another is sold, with the same expiry date but a higher strike price. At expiry, if the stock remains below the lower strike, the position is closed for the difference between the two strike prices. This gives us an overall loss of the initial credit, less this difference. Between the strike prices, the put with the lower strike price will expire worthless. The closing debit on the higher put equals its intrinsic value, so the overall profit is the initial credit less this. If the stock exceeds the higher of the strikes, both puts expire worthless and the initial credit is retained in full. The break-even point of this bull put spread is where the market price equals the higher strike price less the cost of the spread.

The payoffs for the bull call spread and the bull put spread are similar but the bull put spread takes in an initial credit. This can be invested, but margin requirements may be more severe since the lower strike call bought may not cover the put sold. In addition there may be the problem of early exercise.

By selling a call against an otherwise naked call, the investor in the bull call spread is sacrificing an unlimited profit potential in return for decreasing the initial debit. Since the maximum payoff is equal to the difference in strikes, a highly bullish stance is taken by ensuring a small initial debit in an out-of-the-money spread, whereas a less bullish investor would buy an in-the-money spread for lower gearing. The bull call spread is generally regarded as a superior strategy to the bull put spread.

By contrast, bear spreads are the ideal strategy to use when one is bearish of the market in so far as believing that it is more likely to go down than up, but one is not over-enthusiastic about imminent market collapse. As in the bull spreads that we considered, both profit and loss is limited.

For a bear put spread we sell one put and simultaneously purchase a put with the same expiry but at the higher strike price. We can thus establish an initial debit. At expiry if the index remains below the lower strike price, maximum profit is achieved—that of the difference between the strikes less the initial debit. With the index between the strikes, the purchased put is in-the-money while the sold put expires worthless. The total profit is therefore, the intrinsic value of the bought put less the initial debit. If the index exceeds the higher of the strikes, both puts expire worthless and the overall loss is the initial debit of the spread.

As in the bull spread considerations, a position of this nature costs less than the corresponding naked bought put and, therefore has a lower break-even threshold. Profit is restricted to the difference between the two strike prices less the initial debit, but a more bearish investor can choose a small debit and higher gearing by going out-of-the money.

A bear call spread has the same advantages and problems as the bull put spread. The sale of a call together with the purchase of a call with similar expiry but with a higher strike price will generate a net initial credit. However, there will be a margin requirement as the higher strike price bought call may not cover the call sold. Again, there may be the problem of early exercise if the spread is at or in-the-money.

A bear call spread is, of course, exactly the same as a 'sold' bull call spread with the opposite payoff characteristics that we investigated for the bull call spread.

Spread trading summary
BULL CALL SPREAD: buy lower strike call
sell higher strike call
market view bullish
break-even = lower exercise price + net debit
maximum loss = net debit
maximum profit = difference in strikes − net debit

BEAR CALL SPREAD: buy higher strike call
sell lower strike call
market view bearish
break-even = higher exercise price − net credit
maximum loss = difference in strikes − net credit
maximum profit = net credit

BULL PUT SPREAD: buy lower strike put
sell higher strike put
market view bullish
break-even = higher exercise price − net credit
maximum loss = difference in strikes − net credit
maximum profit = net credit

BEAR PUT SPREAD: buy higher strike put
sell lower strike put
market view bearish
break-even = higher exercise price − net debit
maximum loss = net debit
maximum profit = difference in strikes − net debit

2. Precision trades

The most common precision trades are:

- straddles
- strangles
- butterflies
- ratio spreads
- calendar spreads.

Straddles

In our earlier section on volatility we saw that the price of an
option was to a considerable degree governed by its volatility. It
is, therefore, possible to construct a strategy that will allow us to
profit if option prices underestimate the market's volatility. The
investor buys a put and buys a call with the same exercise price
and expiry month. This is called a long straddle. If the index at
expiry remains below the common strike price, then the call
expires worthless but the put is exercised. Profit equals the
intrinsic value of the put less the initial debit (Figure 4.13). When
the index lies at exactly the strike price on expiry, both options
expire worthless and the maximum possible loss, that of the entire
paid premium, is achieved. If the index remains above the strike
price, the put will expire worthless but the call is exercised and
the profit will equal the intrinsic value of the call less the initial
debit.

A straddle is bought when significant movement is expected but
in an unpredictable direction. Because of the high premium paid it
is not common for a straddle to be run to expiry. Time will erode
value rapidly if the expected market movement does not take place.
Under such circumstances the position should either be unwound
or, if a smaller movement is now expected or seen, one side of the
straddle can be closed and a new position opened to turn the

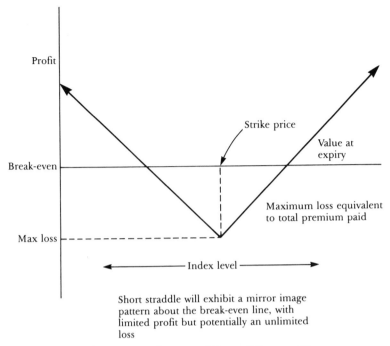

Profit

Strike price

Value at
expiry

Break-even

Maximum loss equivalent
to total premium paid

Max loss

Index level

Short straddle will exhibit a mirror image
pattern about the break-even line, with
limited profit but potentially an unlimited
loss

Figure 4.13 Long straddle profit/loss profile

overall position into that of a bull spread or bear spread. Alternatively, if the index rises strongly, the loss-making put could be sold, and another put with a higher strike price bought. This has the effect of placing us into a 'strangle', but with a locked-in intrinsic value.

Traders looking for volatility to decrease can generate premium income by selling straddles, so long as the risks are accepted.

Strangles
A strangle is similar to a straddle, and again the position is opened when one expects a large market move in one direction or another. The difference is that the calls and puts employed are at different exercise prices and consequently they have much more ambitious break-even points (Figure 4.14). The index must move more significantly for the position to show a profit; on the other hand, they are cheaper to open than straddles.

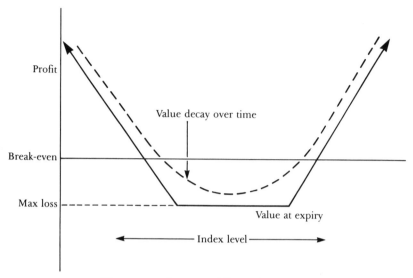

Figure 4.14   Long straddle profit/loss profile

Butterflies

This is a slightly more complex trade than those we have looked at so far. It can be thought of as either a bull spread combined with a bear spread, with staggered strike prices; or as a fully covered, written straddle. To open a butterfly in its own right, three equidistant strike prices are selected for a single expiry date (Figure 4.15). A call is then bought at the highest and lowest of the three strike prices, and two calls are sold at the middle strike price, e.g.:

> buy June 2450 call at 45
>
> sell June 2500 call × 2 at 22 = 44
>
> buy June 2550 call at 8
>
> net initial debit 9

We now have a position where an expiry below the lower strike or above the upper strike price of the butterfly will show a loss equal to the initial debit that we paid. Between the lower and middle strike prices a profit will be seen equal to the intrinsic value of the lower strike price bought call, less the initial debit paid. Above the middle strike price but below the higher strike, the profit realized will be equal to the difference in the intrinsic values of the lowest and middle strike prices, less the initial debit paid.

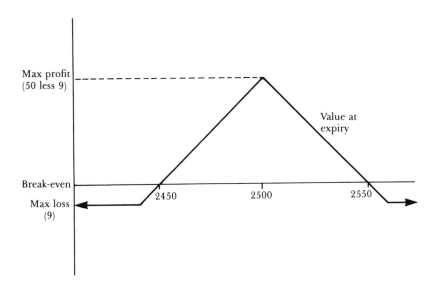

Figure 4.15 Long butterfly example

Except when options prices show anomalies, it will be virtually impossible to open a butterfly position directly in the market at advantageous terms, that is at a zero initial debit or better. A butterfly position will generally develop over a period of time as an accumulation of other positions, such as covering a sold straddle, combining two spreads or covering the unlimited side of a ratio spread. If one takes this approach it is quite possible to enter a butterfly for no debit thus locking-in a potential profit at no risk. It will, of course, mean that we will have been exposed to some degree of market risk in the interim, but this will have been chosen to reflect the expected movement of the market.

Ratio spreads
The reader will by now be aware that by combining the purchases or sales of calls or puts we can develop virtually an infinite set of strategies to cater for every nuance of a view that we may have on the market. Ratio spreads can aid in fine tuning a strategy to a

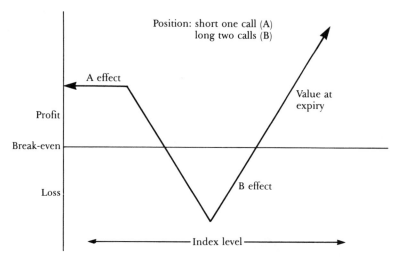

Figure 4.16 Ratio call spread

particular market view or investment strategy requirement. By varying the ratio of calls or puts bought to those sold in spreads, it is possible to create new strategies, still classed as spreads but with different properties. By convention, a written ratio spread, where an initial credit is taken, is generally called a backspread.

For the ratio call spread (Figure 4.16), break-even occurs at the lower strike price plus the initial debit and at twice the higher strike less the lower strike price, less the initial debit. For a put backspread, break-even occurs in a similar manner.

A ratio call spread allows an investor to take a standard call spread and enhance its performance between the strike prices at the expense of theoretically unlimited losses should the market move up very strongly. As there is this exposure, margin requirements will have to be made. A typical ratio call spread buyer will purchase calls (or puts) at or near-the-money and sell calls (or puts) out-of-the-money. The investor is then taking a moderately bullish position (or bearish in the case of puts) which gives a maximum profit at the higher strike price, tailing off sharply if the share price moves further. If the market stagnates, or reverses, the investor will usually keep a small initial credit.

The ratio of options sold or bought is generally 2:1, but investors can use other combinations like 3:2, 5:3 or even 3:1. The more extreme ratios will perform better if the market moves as hoped, but will have a much earlier cut-off point leading into a far steeper loss-making situation.

Calendar spreads
Calendar spreads are a particular strategy that hopes to capitalize on the relatively slow rate of time decay in long-dated options compared to short-dated ones.

The normal way to capitalize on this is to purchase long-dated options and sell short-dated options against them. This will create an initial debit but as time passes and the shorter option nears expiry the differential between the two options should widen, showing us, hopefully, a profit. The long-dated option does have to be closed on expiry of the short-dated one for the investor to avoid market risk. Alternatively, the long-dated option can instead be used as part of a new strategy.

Calendar spreads may be established with either call or put options. At expiry of the short-dated option, maximum profit will be shown if the index is at the common strike price. At this level the sold option will expire worthless. If the index is higher then the sold option will gain value, because of the delta factor, faster than the bought option, with the result that the position loses value overall. If the index falls the sold option is still worthless, but the long-dated bought option will be losing value.

Although the calendar spread strategy is designed to capitalize on time decay it can be upset by movements in the index level. Normally, both options would equally reflect market movements but at times, particularly near expiry, one may be affected much more than the other. To provide some protection, the mutual strike price should be selected to lie as close as possible to the investor's expectation of the future index level.

3.   Locked trades and synthetics

There are many index trading strategies using stock index futures contracts in conjunction with stock index options that create a variety of risk-return profiles. When using stock index options and futures contracts of the same size, like the CAC-40 at FF200 times its index both for the option and the future or the Swedish OMX 30 at SEK 100 times the index again both for its option and its future, compatability is built in. In the UK, the futures contract trades at £25 times the index, the option at £10 times the index, so matching positions will require an options to futures ratio of 5:2.

Synthetic options strategies involve the combination of an options position with an offsetting futures market position and are intended to produce near risk-free arbitrages designed to profit from anomalies in the pricing of options and futures.

Synthetic index future

Earlier we mentioned the rather aggressive strategy of buying calls and selling puts. In fact this strategy duplicates the behaviour of a long position in the index future. In order to go long, the investor purchases a call and sells a put of the same expiry date and strike price. Usually this will result in a net initial debit.

At expiry, if the index is below the common strike price, the call will expire worthless but the put will be assigned. At the strike price both options expire worthless while above the strike price, the put will expire worthless but the investor will exercise the call. In any case, the investor effectively buys the index at the strike price plus the net premium paid (initial debit). The initial premium paid may be modified by moving the selected strike price. This will tend to shift cost from the premium to the strike price, or vice versa.

Since synthetics are one of the standard methods used to hedge positions, the creation of a competitively priced example (against the futures) should be quite rare. When it does appear possible, other than when the futures contract is exhibiting anomalous basis trading, the investor should be aware of the possibility of early exercise on one half of the synthetic future.

The sale of a synthetic at one strike price against another synthetic purchased at a different strike price creates a 'box' strategy. This guarantees a profit if the net credit taken exceeds the difference in strike prices. Early exercise again may, however, be a problem.

Conversion and reversal

These are similar strategies as both involve a position in the futures contract and an opposite via the synthetic future.

A 'conversion' involves the sale of a synthetic future against a futures purchase, i.e.

buy 1 futures contract	at 2450
sell 1 call 2450	at 50
buy 1 put 2450	at 30
net initial debit	2430

Below the mutual strike price, the investor sells the index via exercise of the put. This gives him a net profit of the strike price minus the initial debit. The sold call expires worthless. At the strike, he merely sells the stock again locking in the same profit. Above the strike price, the sold call is assigned and the put bought expires worthless. This again locks the investor into a profit equal to the strike price less the initial debit. In each case the profit is the difference between the sold call and the purchased put. This example may seem attractive, but it must be remembered that we are looking at an arbitrage exercise and consequently an opportunity that will only arise in an imperfect market. Normally, such opportunities are very rare. A constant worry in a situation where this transaction may be possible is that of premature exercise by the counterparty of one side of our synthetic. For this reason some investors may prefer to use a 'cylinder'. This is much the same as a synthetic but both options selected are out-of-money. This will reduce the risk of early exercise considerably but will not allow a strict conversion to be created.

The opposite of a conversion is a reversion or reversal and is characterized by:

- selling a put
- buying a call with the same exercise
- selling a futures contract.

We open a synthetic long position and close it through a short futures position.

Is it all worth while?

Many investors can be forgiven for thinking that all these theoretical strategies are all very well from an academic point of view, but are they really worth while in practice? Surely all successful investment hinges on the fact that if something is going up we should have the required wherewithal to be adequately long of it—and if not, we should not be in the business of managing money. One might understand the occasional purchase of a call or put option, but synthetics take investment into abstract spheres; options in isolation as well as futures markets are in any case a zero sum game, just like a colossal game of gin-rummy (with a net dealing cost to the man who shuffles the cards—the broker, the only one who constantly thinks all this is a good idea.)

Answering such comments, often made in a spirit of frustration, with consolation and logic, 'yes' the game, if one is flippant enough to call it such, is a zero sum. But that is missing the point of the whole essence of derivative products. In utilizing futures and options we are not indulging in some random redistribution of wealth, we are seeking to manage risk in the most efficient way possible. These markets allow the transfer of risk from those who do not want it to those who do. So many different funds now exist that one investor may have considerable worries about the market rising, while another will spend sleepless nights considering the implications of a market collapse. One man's insurance premium is another man's speculative profit. More and more funds now look for added value not through improved share selection, but by the skilful use of options, futures and warrants, by prudent risk management techniques, and by pushing the statistical advantage just a little bit further in one's favour.

While we may not actually start our strategy by deciding to open a synthetic arbitrage position, the fact that we know that we can create all sorts of profitable or statistically advantageous positions, gives us the added flexibility to develop such positions in a constantly changing market.

Stock index options or futures

Some investors, once involved with derivative instruments, gravitate to using one or another, almost entirely to the exclusion of the other instruments. This is not an ideal situation. Options, futures and warrants should not be regarded as competing instruments, all fighting for a share of a particular strategy, but as complementary, each able to provide particular advantages under specific circumstances.

Investors wishing to buy the market can, of course, use options or futures. Buying the future instantly puts the investor long of the market at a price that may or may not be in line with fair-value. An option, on the other hand, can be more selective. Although the futures basis will generally be reflected in the options premium, we can decide on our degree of commitment to the market by selecting our strike price. Out-of-the-money strikes will be cheaper, but the options may expire worthless. In-the-money strikes may or may not be cheaper to futures contracts and provide almost the same degree of commitment to a bullish position. Very large positions are likely to be easier to put on in the futures market as it is often the case that a professional option seller will use the futures market as a hedge for his own position.

For investors with total funds not available for immediate use, both futures and options provide an opportunity to gear up. In the futures market, the gearing is set by the margin requirement against the underlying value of the contract, but we deal at the quoted price. Options let us choose our degree of gearing exactly the same as choosing the degree of risk that we are prepared to accept, but in each case we have to pay a premium, the cost of owning an option.

For this reason, dealing via the futures contract will always be cheaper. Futures and options finally differ only in the obvious; one is a commitment, long or short; the second is the right to choose— and that costs money; and, finally, for the option seller the position is similar to the holder of a future, except that the degree of risk will change as the market moves.

Index warrants

Over the last few years, index warrants have come to be regarded as very important derivative instruments by which exposure to an equity market may be amended.

An index warrant gives its owner the right to buy or sell, depending on whether the warrant is a call or put warrant, the underlying index at a fixed level, on or before a fixed date. In this respect, an index warrant is no different to an index option, but in contrast to an option, warrants are issued with a much longer life, generally between two and five years. The other major difference is that warrants are not traded on specific exchanges. Instead they are 'issued' by certain institutions, mainly highly rated banks.

These issuers, while having to guarantee performance on expiry of the warrant, generally undertake to make a secondary market in the warrants. Some issuing houses undertake to make a secondary market in any of the warrants that they issue with a guaranteed dealing spread and minimum size of quotation. As warrants are not traded as visibly as on an open outcry market, warrant buyers must satisfy themselves that they will be able to close their positions on reasonable quotations at any time that they wish to do so. Index warrants are now available for all the major equity markets (USA, Japan, UK, France and Germany) and tend to be priced in the domestic currency of the country, although it is quite possible to alter the quoted currency at the wish of the warrant buyer.

As with options, warrants will be either 'European' or 'American' exercise. 'European' exercise means that the warrant holder can only exercise on the expiry day of the warrant. If the warrant has 'American' exercise then it can be exercised at any time up to the moment of expiry.

Comparison of FT-SE 100 Index warrants (by expiry date) is given in Table 4.2. The listing of the various FT-SE 100 Index warrants available at a particular moment in time illustrates the various aspects that one must consider. Expiry dates and strike prices are straightforward, the other details need some clarification.

Warrant ratios

The warrant index ratio, shown variously as 1, 10 or 100 denotes the number of warrants needed to represent the index, i.e. 1, 10 or 100. As a result, the warrant price must be multiplied by 10 or 100 in order to get a true costing of the investment. There really is no reason why warrants should be 'decimated' in this manner other than for the cosmetic reasons of making a warrant look cheaper, and then giving the trader the mental kudos of dealing in very large numbers!

Break-even levels

Break-even levels, as with options, are calculated for put warrants as the strike price less the price of the warrant; for call warrants the break-even is the strike price plus the cost of the warrant.

Premiums

Warrant premium is the measure usually used to determine the attractiveness of a warrant. While it is preferable to always buy a particular warrant at as low a premium as possible, it is not always a simple matter to identify the relatively cheapest warrant on offer.

Percentage premium of a call warrant is calculated as follows:

$$P\% = \left(\frac{WP + SP - IL}{IL}\right) \times 100$$

where P   = premium
       WP = warrant price
       SP = strike price
       IL = index level

The warrant price for the purposes of the calculation will have been adjusted by the warrant-index ratio to equate to one index unit. If a warrant is out-of-the-money, in other words it has no intrinsic value, the index will by definition be lower than the strike price (for a call warrant). Under such circumstances it will be impossible to buy the call warrant at a nil premium. To illustrate, if the current index level is at 2000 and the strike level is 2500, with the warrant price at zero the percentage premium will be:

$$\left(\frac{0 + 2500 - 2000}{2000}\right) \times 100 = 25\%$$

This example shows that any out-of-the-money warrant will have a minimum premium equal to the percentage that the exercise price exceeds the index level. It is, therefore, not a valid argument to say that warrants with a percentage premium above 20 per cent are expensive and those below are cheap. Degrees of out-of-the-moneyness have to be considered as well.

Put warrant premiums are calculated in a similar fashion, but the formula is amended to:

$$\left(\frac{WP - SP + IL}{IL}\right) \times 100$$

Gearing
This is sometimes also known as the 'capital ratio', and is calculated as:

$$\frac{\text{index level}}{\text{warrant price} \times \text{ratio}}$$

The higher the warrant price in relation to the index level, the lower the gearing, and as the warrant price decreases, gearing will increase. Again it is not always easy to compare like with like when similar gearings on two different warrants may in fact be separated by vastly different strike prices and expiry dates. For this reason, gearing is sometimes calculated as the warrant price as a ratio of the strike level.

Delta or hedge ratio

The delta of a warrant is a measure of the sensitivity of the warrant price to changes in the underlying index. As with options, delta

Table 4.2 Comparison of FT-SE 100 Index warrants by expiry date

Index: 2509.1

FT-SE 100 put warrants   18 June 1991

Issuer	Expiry date	Life (yrs)	Strike price	Wnt/ idx	Price £	%-age prem.	Break- even	Grng
Mitsubishi	20–Aug–91	0.2	2378	1	75.00	8.2%	2303	33.5
Bankers Trust	27–Sep–91	0.3	1730	1	2.10	31.1%	1728	1194.8
Paribas	30–Sep–91	0.3	2080	10	0.43	17.3%	2076	583.5
Bankers Trust	28–Nov–91	0.4	1730	1	3.90	31.2%	1726	643.4
Citibank	18–Dec–91	0.5	1750	100	0.09	30.6%	1741	278.8
Soc. Gen.	31–Dec–91	0.5	2070	10	1.79	18.2%	2052	140.2
Soc. Gen.	31–Mar–92	0.8	2059	10	2.96	19.1%	2029	84.8
Bankers Trust	31–Mar–92	0.8	2396	10	11.30	9.0%	2283	22.2
Soc. Gen.	30–Jun–92	1.0	1800	10	1.13	28.7%	1789	222.0
Soc. Gen.	30–Jun–92	1.0	2000	10	2.26	21.2%	1977	111.0
Soc. Gen.	30–Jun–92	1.0	2200	10	5.28	14.4%	2147	47.5
BZW	29–Sep–92	1.3	1800	100	0.14	28.8%	1786	179.2
BZW	29–Sep–92	1.3	1900	100	0.19	25.0%	1881	132.1
BZW	29–Sep–92	1.3	2000	100	0.25	21.3%	1975	100.4
BZW	29–Sep–92	1.3	2100	100	0.31	17.5%	2069	80.9
BZW	29–Sep–92	1.3	2200	100	0.48	14.2%	2152	52.3
BZW	29–Sep–92	1.3	2300	100	0.72	11.2%	2228	34.8
BZW	29–Sep–92	1.3	2400	100	1.03	8.5%	2297	24.4
Citibank	29–Sep–92	1.3	2130	100	0.39	16.7%	2091	64.3
Citibank	16–Dec–92	1.5	1750	100	0.16	30.9%	1734	156.8
Citibank	16–Dec–92	1.5	1950	100	0.20	23.1%	1930	125.5
Citibank	25–Mar–93	1.8	2300	100	0.96	12.2%	2204	26.1
Citibank	25–Mar–93	1.8	2500	100	1.60	6.7%	2340	15.7
Bankers Trust	30–Mar–93	1.8	2280	1	122.00	14.0%	2158	20.6
Citibank	15–Dec–93	2.5	1850	100	0.35	27.7%	1815	71.7
Bankers Trust	31–Mar–94	2.8	2458.5	10	20.5	10.2%	2254	12.2

FT-SE 100 call warrants

Issuer	Expiry date	Life (yrs)	Strike price	Wnt/ idx	Price £	%-age prem.	Break- even	Grng
Fleming	09–Dec–91	0.5	1600	1	940.00	1.2%	2540	2.7
Soc. Gen.	31–Dec–91	0.5	2280	10	32.60	3.9%	2606	7.7
Soc. Gen.	31–Mar–92	0.8	2059	10	51.50	2.6%	2574	4.9
Soc. Gen.	30–Jun–92	1.0	2000	10	60.00	3.6%	2600	4.2
Soc. Gen.	30–Jun–92	1.0	2200	10	45.40	5.8%	2654	5.5
Soc. Gen.	30–Jun–92	1.0	2400	10	32.30	8.5%	2723	7.8
BZW	29–Sep–92	1.3	2000	100	6.24	4.6%	2624	4.0
BZW	29–Sep–92	1.3	2100	100	5.48	5.5%	2648	4.6
BZW	29–Sep–92	1.3	2200	100	4.75	6.6%	2675	5.3
BZW	29–Sep–92	1.3	2300	100	4.08	7.9%	2708	6.1
BZW	29–Sep–92	1.3	2400	100	3.47	9.5%	2747	7.2
BZW	29–Sep–92	1.3	2500	100	2.92	11.3%	2792	8.6
Citibank	30–Sep–92	1.3	2130	100	5.50	6.8%	2680	4.6
Citibank	25–Mar–93	1.8	2500	100	3.66	14.2%	2866	6.9
Citibank	25–Mar–93	1.8	2700	100	2.67	18.2%	2967	9.4
Bankers Trust	31–Mar–94	2.8	2458.5	10	51.00	18.3%	2969	4.9

varies between 0 and 1 for call warrants and 0 and −1 for put warrants. The further out-of-the-money a warrant is, the closer is the delta to 0 because changes in the underlying index have little effect on the value of the warrant. Warrants deeply in-the-money have deltas closer to 1, or −1 for put warrants because the absolute changes in share and warrant price are similar.

Leverage
As mentioned earlier, 'gearing' can lead to confusion in that it may mean different things to different investors. Leverage is a slightly different concept that uses delta in its considerations. It is defined as:

$$\frac{\text{delta} \times \text{index level}}{\text{warrant price } (\times \text{ratio})}$$

Leverage is in fact the expected percentage price change of a warrant for a 1 per cent change in the price of the underlying index. In many ways it is a better measure than gearing.

Valuation of warrants
Ultimate valuation of index warrants is carried out in exactly the same manner as index options, i.e. by using the mathematical

model developed by Black & Scholes, or amended versions of the
B & S model.

Reasons for using index warrants

1. Warrants can give investors considerable leverage.
2. The normally long life of warrants will allow long-term strategic
   investment decisions to be made, at transaction costs that are
   lower than those of constantly rolling forward short-term
   options.
3. As with options, holders of warrants will know their costs, i.e.
   they will have limited downside liability, but unlimited profit
   potential.

One of the reasons why so many different warrants are now
available in many diverse markets, is that, aside from their obvious
strategic use by institutional investors, they can also be extremely
profitable to the issuing parties. They use their expertise to create
a financial instrument that is then sold to the consumer on a cost
plus, or more realistically in this case, on a risk plus basis. The
issuing houses skills are utilized in creating a hedging strategy to
underwrite the issued warrants. The warrant buyer pays for this
via the warrant premium.

Warrants can readily be created on any market where the
issuing house can utilize options, futures or even the underlying
equities themselves for the construction of their own dynamic
hedging strategies that eliminate the underwriting risk. Increasing
awareness of the techniques used in issuing warrants is leading to
many more houses acting as issuers, and as a result premiums are
becoming more competitive. We can even see the next stage
developing where larger fund managers, instead of buying warrants, develop the same techniques used in warrant creation in
order to construct their own dynamic hedge strategies or geared
investment programmes for in-house requirements. Buying a warrant is after all paying a premium for someone else's ability to
provide a 'packaged' longer term hedge or investment policy. This
is good value to those investors who need a ready-made or bespoke
investment vehicle that will save them time and effort (as in some
overseas markets that they may not fully research), but warrants
can be very expensive to the larger, more sophisticated house,

which should be utilizing dynamic investment strategies as a matter of course. On the other hand, warrant issuers seek to launch warrants with the greatest potential appeal, and if sufficient demand is identified, warrants can be specially created to meet specific strike level and expiry period requirements.

Some problems of using index warrants

1. The market may not be as liquid as an options or futures market.
2. Warrants can be more expensive. They are priced on higher implied volatilities in order to provide extra comfort to the warrant issuers.
3. Dealing prices are not as visible as in 'open outcry' or other exchange regulated markets.
4. The range of available strike prices and expiry dates is limited relative to options.
5. Some investors may not be allowed to use non-exchange traded products—even if the integrity of the underwriters is assured.

CHAPTER 5

The mechanics of trading

A first glance into a futures dealing pit gives one the impression of total chaos—happening rapidly. There are large numbers of dealers in bright jackets shouting at each other in coded terms while waving their arms around in equally bewildering gestures. But there is meaning to everything. What we are actually seeing is a highly efficient and highly organized market place, and as in all market places, buyers and sellers are brought together in order to trade. In the case of 'open outcry' options and futures markets (we shall look briefly at electronic markets later), the deal struck on the floor of the exchange is just a small part of the overall action; there is much more than meets the eye going on before, after and all around.

The progress of an order

Everything starts with the buyer and the seller. Whether the initiator is a private investor seeking a speculative return or a major institution looking to commit large public funds to a particular investment strategy, it is their decision to trade that starts a whole chain of events. The client will normally give a dealing order to a broker, with whom a legal agreement to trade will have first been signed. Because of the geared nature of futures and options contracts, brokers have a legal obligation to formally explain to new clients the risks associated with these instruments, and satisfy themselves that the client is aware of what obligations they are entering into. The client should, of course, select his or her broker with regard to what the client needs from the relationship. Many broking houses will provide research and supporting services as well as the execution of orders. Under these circumstances the relationship between client and broker may become more of a team effort in deciding how to approach particular investment strategies. Other houses, sometimes known as discount brokers, will provide a no frills execution only service and generally charge a lower commission. One gets what one pays for, and one should only pay for what one needs. Cheap commissions can, however, prove costly if they result in bad executions.

Once the client has confirmed the order with his broker, the broker will pass it to his floor dealer for execution. He may use his own 'in-house' dealer or an independent 'local' acting on his behalf. The coloured jackets of the floor dealers aid them to identify with which company they have struck a bargain.

Trading on the exchange takes place by means of 'open outcry' in a particular 'pit' or area where a certain contract is traded. Bids and offers with the volume that a dealer is prepared to trade are made audibly to all other members in the pit. Acceptance of a bid or an offer must also be clearly heard. Inferior bids or offers may not be made to those currently shown in the pit. Pit observers, employed by the exchange, monitor all trading during the day, enforce dealing rules and administer trading regulations.

Exchanges go to great lengths to ensure that all trading is both fair and seen to be fair as the success of a particular contract and, consequently also the exchange, is in no small way dependent on a public perception that trading is carried out honestly. All trades, bids and offers, together with the market volume, are continuously transmitted via the exchange's display boards to the various real-time worldwide quotation systems such as Reuters, Telerate, etc.

On receipt of an order from the client, the order is transmitted to the floor-dealing team who enter details of the order on a dealing slip and time-stamp it. The order is then passed by runner or hand signal to the dealer in the pit for execution.

Once the order is filled, either by runner or hand signal, this is communicated back to the order taker who enters the details on the dealing slip, and again time-stamps it. Confirmation is made back to the broker and then the client. Although the procedure involves many steps, a client placing an order can have an

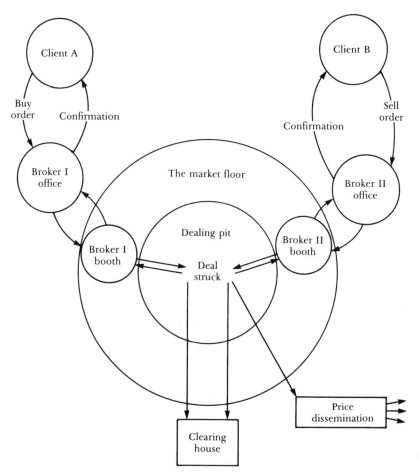

Figure 5.1   Order flow

execution confirmed back in seconds if dealing is being transacted through 'open' telephone lines.

Completed trading slips, which also show counterparty details, are given up to the clearing house for entry into a computerized matching and registration system. All trades must be matched by the end of the day and confirmed trades are published by the clearing house. The general flow of an order from initiation to execution and confirmation is shown in Figure 5.1.

Once the deal is done, the two counterparties submit the trade to the clearing house for matching and confirmation. Although the deal is struck between two member firms, in each case the contract

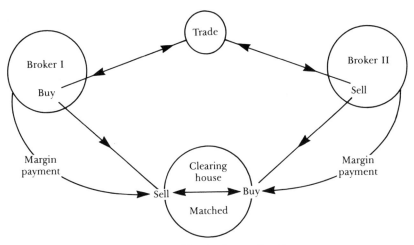

Figure 5.2 Clearing house function

is between the broker and the clearing house, as well as the original contract between the client and the broker.

The clearing house

The concept of a 'clearing house' goes back to the origin of formal futures contracts, and in one form or another they are to be found wherever an exchange operates (Figure 5.2). Their function is simple: to eliminate, as far as possible, the risk that someone at some stage will not be able to honour their bargains, with the possibility that a bad debt domino effect could wipe out many of the exchanges participants as well as their clients. Clearing house members are, therefore, usually the most financially secure firms of an exchange. In some countries, the clearing house may ultimately be government backed. In every case the business of the exchange must be separated from the independent nature of the clearing house function.

The London Clearing House, which is responsible for the clearing of contracts traded on LIFFE, traces its origins to 1888 when as the London Produce Clearing House it cleared contracts and guaranteed good delivery on coffee and sugar. Now the London Clearing House, part of the International Commodities Clearing House (ICCH), is owned by six of London's largest clearing banks: National Westminster, Barclays, Midland and

Lloyds each with a 20 per cent share; Standard Chartered and the Royal Bank of Scotland each with 10 per cent. It is backed by guarantees of £150 million.

The role of a clearing house can be summarized as follows:

1. It provides central clearing, thereby ensuring that all members of the exchange actually fulfil their obligations. As member contracts are with the exchange, counterparty credit risk is largely eliminated.
2. It acts as a central bank to all exchange members by matching all trades transacted on the exchange floor.
3. It sets margin levels and handles movements in margin requirements.
4. It undertakes the responsibility for the good delivery of each contract, thereby guaranteeing trades.

The clearing house protects itself by demanding initial margin on an opening transaction and operates a system of daily variation margins, thereby maintaining for itself a balanced book. Members of the exchange similarly require margin deposits from their clients. Only members that are clearing members of the exchange may deal directly with the clearing house. Non-clearing members have to clear their trades through a clearing member.

Types of order and their placement

The terminology employed in the futures markets differs from that used in the cash markets to a considerable degree. Many more terms are employed, and it is vital that correct and clearly understood orders are given in what are often fast moving markets. Miscommunication is one of the greatest sources of costly errors.

It is as well to know how to place 'buy' or 'sell' orders correctly before we get involved in order qualifications. For buying, the accepted order of words is 'Pay (price) for (quantity)' which may be, 'pay 20 for 6'. Doubtless there will be some numbers before the 20, but if the market is quoted 19–21 it is accepted that the index real level of 2519–2521 is the one that we are trading—and not 2420! The onus is on the order giver to know the big figure at which he thinks he is dealing.

When selling, the correct form is 'sell (quantity) at (price)' or say 'sell 6 at 20'. The human brain often does not hear the first word of a spoken sentence, consequently a rapidly given 'pay' or 'sell' may be missed. However, as the terminology is established, 'for' becomes synonymous with a purchase order and the word 'at' with a sell order. Some dealers even go so far as to avoid using the terms 'pay' or 'sell', settling instead for '20 for 6' or '6 at 20'.

Market order   This is the most common type of order and is a straightforward instruction to buy or sell 'at market' or 'at best', i.e. the price prevailing at the time. If the size of the order is larger than the volume currently available in the dealing pit, then executions are unlikely to be all at the same price as the dealer will have to bid up or offer down until he secures the desired volume. Large 'at market' orders will, therefore, have a tendency of moving the market against the order giver and thus tend to be used by large participants who are either not oversensitive to price movements or who in fact wish to move the market in a particular direction.

Limit order   This is an order to buy or sell at a specified price, or better than the specified price. A limit order puts more responsibility on the dealer since he must be aware of his limit orders and trade them once his limit is reached. An order to 'sell 6 at 20' stops the offer price in the trading pit from rising above '20' until the order is filled. A better offer, say at 19 or 18, would put our 20 offer outside the current market quotation, so the dealer would hold it 'in his pocket' either until the market again rises or the client decides to change the order. The advantage of limit orders is that they are far less likely to push prices in an adverse direction. If it is thought that there is sufficient market force in the opposite direction at current prices then a limit order is feasible. However, in certain market conditions a few ticks 'discretion' from current levels may be appropriate to enable the order to be worked without revealing to the trading pit the size of the order.

Stop-loss orders   These are orders designed to close out positions when a specified price level trades. Once the specified price level is reached or penetrated, the order becomes a 'market order'. Stop-loss orders are a useful discipline for investors wishing to stop more losses once a particular loss (or level of pain!) has been reached. Under orderly market conditions they fill this requirement very well. It must be remembered, though, that an order to 'sell or stop at 2518' with the market trading at 2525 is no guarantee of a totally relaxed existence. It may well be that 2520 is perceived to be a major support level, and once breached with a trade at 2519 this may trigger large numbers of 'sell at market' orders. The buyers sensing desperate sellers may pull back their bids to far lower levels, so the next trade below 2519 may be at 2514 triggering our stop, which then gets executed at the next best level of 2507 in a thin, rapidly collapsing market. While the client may not be overjoyed at this fill to his order it may well be better than having no stop in the market and watching the index decline a further 50 points. A final frustration of stop orders is that often they are triggered, only then to see the market recover. Here there is little that one can do or say in consolation. The point becomes philosophical. Some traders never use stops because, 1. whenever stops get hit the market recovers, and 2. when the market is really collapsing, stops provide no protection as fills tend to be way below desired levels (remember October 1987). Contrary to this somewhat cynical view there are many traders who would never dream of opening a position without a stop on the grounds that while not perfect, it is the best discipline that one can employ in order to protect one's capital. As well as limiting losses, 'buy on stop' or 'sell on stop' orders can be used to protect profitable positions or even to open new market positions once predetermined levels have traded.

Stop limit order In order to get over some of the problems of straight stop orders, a client can place a stop order at a particular level with a limit beyond which the market would not be 'chased'. 'Sell on stop at 2637 limit 35'. Here, once the market declines and trades or is offered at 2637, the dealer will look to sell the position but will not sell below 2635. An order of this nature will not force the market away from the limit, but is in danger of not getting filled at all.

Not held This is a term used when giving the pit dealer some discretion to trade an order when a particular level has been reached. For example, 'sell 20 at 2637 not held' means the dealer may in his judgement not trade immediately at that level if he believes that prices will rise further. There is, however, no guarantee of superior performance with this type of order. The dealer has been given discretion to improve on the desired level, but cannot be held responsible if the market suddenly reverses and the order is not filled at all.

Day order or good for the day   This means just what it says. The limit or stop order will lapse at the end of the dealing day if it has not been enacted during the day.

Good-till-cancelled or GTC   This order remains valid until either filled or cancelled. It is as well to keep record of such orders and monitor them on a daily basis.

Fill-or-kill   An order for immediate transaction. If not filled immediately it must be withdrawn. This order is often used by a party wishing to take out a large bid or offer, but if this cannot be achieved then they do not wish to be seen as a possible large counterparty in the market.

Market if touched or MIT   This order becomes an order to deal 'at market', once a predetermined price has traded in the market.

Basis orders   These orders have two main areas—firstly, to place an order to trade the differential between two futures or options contracts i.e. 'buy June sell September at a differential of 65 points' (see section on spread trading in Chapter 3). A second major use of basis orders is to buy or sell a futures contract at a specified level to the cash index. The index may be standing at 2620 and the future generally trading at a 40-point premium. The investor may wish to buy the future only if he can pay 25 points premium or less over the cash market, i.e. if the cash market trades at 2618 we could pay 2643 on the future. Orders of this nature are usually placed by fund managers seeking to add value to an index fund.

Electronic trading

Some of the new European derivatives markets have never seen an 'open outcry' futures or options exchange, preferring to start with the modern development, the screen-based electronic market. Other markets, like the London Traded Options Market, are contemplating converting from open outcry to electronic. In essence there is little difference to the net result, and where in Figure 5.1 we see the broker booths and the trading pit, we simply replace this with interconnected screen-based broker dealing terminals (Figure 5.3).

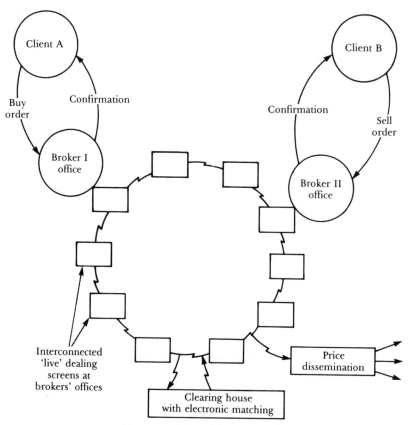

Figure 5.3 The electronic market

On LIFFE this form of trading is available for several contracts or at certain times and is known in London as automated pit trading (APT).

After the open outcry market in FT-SE 100 Index futures has closed, it is still possible to trade in the contract through APT. This operates from 4.32 pm until 5.30 pm and bids, offers and latest dealing prices are transmitted in the same manner as with the open outcry market. Trading is, however, carried on by interlinked 'active' computer screens operated from a number of brokers' offices. Bids and offers, their sizes and originators, are displayed on a screen. When buy and sell levels meet, deals are struck electronically.

Although formal trading on the International Stock Exchange ceases at 4.30 pm, there are several reasons why APT is in demand

and volumes of trading are likely to grow. Firstly, APT allows investors to react to market-sensitive information that may only become apparent after the London market officially ends. Thus, at times of increased volatility, either generated from events in the UK or the USA, the extra dealing period allows traders to hedge exposed positions or back a new market view.

Dealings in American Depositary Receipts (ADRs), the instruments for trading UK equities in the US markets, can also now be partially hedged on the FT-SE Index, as the available ADR's account for over 75 per cent of the capitalization of the index.

Many 'more traditional' dealers have very little love for electronic trading systems, believing with some justification that machines are replacing traders. Dealing is being reduced to the level of a computer game. There is understandably considerable nostalgia for the old days when deals were proposed eye to eye, while watching for signs of a furrowed brow or a nervous lump in the throat, and finally agreed over a handshake.

It can be expected that open outcry markets will always survive in some form, but electronic trading is now seen to be a natural development that can be expected to grow more and more as the world develops truly international and interconnected market places. The global markets of the future will be electronic markets with intercontinental dealing points.

CHAPTER 6

Technical analysis and the index markets

The dedicated technical analyst does not want his mind clouded by any facts of a fundamental nature, believing instead that by considering past price movements, future price movements can be predicted with a degree of statistical certainty. There are many sceptics about who write the entire science off as little better than astrology or spodomancy (the divination of the future by watching the way ash crumbles), pointing out that there are now so many facets to technical analysis, as well as so many analysts, that somebody somewhere will always be able to claim 'it works, I got it right!'

Possibly this scepticism, that is more of a European characteristic than an American one, has rather constrained the spread of technical analysts in Europe. The main UK and European broking and investment houses all have significant commitments to fundamental analysis departments. Technical analysts tend to be far more thinly spread and in some areas are still regarded with suspicion—not least because if perchance technical analysis is seen to work, it is far cheaper to employ one technician to look at all the charts of the investments in which we are interested, than to employ several highly paid fundamental analysts, each with expertise in their own narrow fields.

Even so, the growing membership list in the UK of the Society of Technical Analysts confirms the increasing acceptance that technical analysis has an important role to play as part of the information required in any investment decision. In the USA, technical analysis has been given a far higher profile for some very good, historical reasons. Charles Dow, through developing his stock market averages, led in turn to index charts and their consideration. William Hamilton, who succeeded Dow as editor of the *Wall Street Journal*, developed these ideas further into 'barometers of business conditions'. Prices were seen to have major and minor trends. Other researchers looked for chart guidance, particularly after the much publicized success of R. N. Elliott's wave cycles; and more particularly the astounding successes of W. D. Gann who used only technical analysis to amass a huge fortune in a relatively short space of time. Since then the USA has been very much regarded as the home of technical analysis and there is no great surprise to note that technical analysts are employed in proportionately far greater numbers by American institutions than anywhere else in the world. Many funds are also now run purely on the basis of technical input—which lends itself comfortably to adaptation into countless computer models.

Sceptics may still not be convinced, but must concede that with so much technical analysis being carried out, the technicians themselves are apt to become, at significant moments, a market force, and thus cannot be ignored. It is also worth remembering that technical analysis, just like the rules of speculation, is ultimately a discipline. Both have similar messages. The rules of speculation may tell us not to go against the trend, a simple observation no doubt learnt by many through their own costly mistakes. The technician will inform us that the market is in a downward channel and that no buy signals are currently evident. At the most sophisticated level, technical analysts are using extremely complex considerations, and believe that their mathematics can give us an insight into the science of mass psychology. While there still can be some legitimate question in investors minds over the value of recognizing some of the more obscure chart patterns, understanding of trends, changes in trading volume and open interest, and market momentum are all technical considerations of vital importance in the timing of trades. The possibility has to be acknowledged that technical analysis gives us a scientific interpretation of successful 'gut-feel'.

Finding the trend

A quick look at any chart will indicate times when the market is going one way or the other. Whenever the market is making

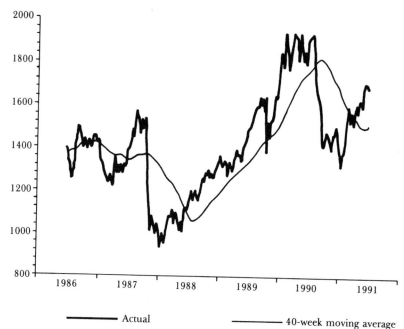

Figure 6.1 Bull and bear phases of the Deutsche Aktien (DAX)
Price Index

Source: Datastream plc, 1991. Reproduced with permission

higher highs and higher lows on the setbacks, the trend is upwards. Lower lows and lower highs indicate a downtrend. This approach will give us a first impression of overall market trend. Closer inspection will show that within this trend are smaller trends, and within those should we have the necessary charts we could identify the two or three minute trends so favoured by the pit traders.

The major trend is generally accepted to last for several months or even years, generally indicating whether the market is in long term bull or bear mode (Figure 6.1). While no overall definition of a major trend has been generally accepted, one useful and simple guide is to look at the closing prices of the index against the 200-day moving average (simply the average of the last 200 days of closing prices). If the index is above the average, we are in a bull market, if below, then a bear market.

Long-term investment decisions should be consistent with the major trend of the index that we are trading. Intermediate trends are the next shortest and generally run from one to four months, occasionally a little longer. These are identified by charting weekly closing prices. Normally, two lower or two higher weekly closes after a run in a particular direction should alert the investor that the intermediate trend may be changing. These intermediate trends are important for the long-term investor seeking optimum timing for his investments as well as for the three-month-view speculator.

Minor trends are the most volatile. They tend to be the least predictable, but when they do develop they are the steepest of all. Large profits or losses can be seen very quickly. Normally these minor trends only last for up to 30 days. Greatest difficulty lies in making sure that one is on the right side of a minor trend. It is all too easy to think we have a trend only to find that we actually have an oscillation that causes a financially painful whiplash every other day. A simple discipline is to consider the day's trading range over a three-day period. Progressive higher highs and higher lows could indicate the start of a minor uptrend. Two days of the opposite, and the uptrend may have been negated. A disciplined approach like this will avoid the danger of running a large loss. A small investor may, however, be bled white by the accumulation of a surfeit of minor 'whiplash losses'.

Types of chart

In order to make interpretations, the technical analyst can use several different types of chart. Each will have slightly different characteristics that are useful in the visual representation of stock index behaviour.

Bar chart

A bar chart is one of the most widely used charts (Figure 6.2). The market movement is recorded on a daily basis as a vertical line between the high and low, the closing level being indicated as a horizontal dash. As well as a daily record, similar charts can be drawn for weekly or monthly price ranges. Although bar charts (also referred to as high-low-close charts) are the most popular for technical analysts, their minor limitation is that they do not show how the market acted during the trading day. It may have taken

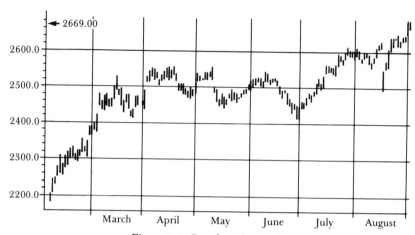

Figure 6.2   Bar chart for FT-SE
Source: Pont Data, 1990. Reproduced with permission

the whole day to establish the trading range or it may have been a very active market oscillating throughout the day and reaching the highs and lows several times.

Line chart

A line chart is the simplest chart, and generally drawn by the non-technical investor interested in getting a quick visual impression of the general movement of the market. Normally closing prices are used and are joined to form a line chart. They are not really adequate for market movement interpretation, but can give a very good indication as to what the market has been doing over a longer time scale, up to 10 or 20 years. For technical analysts their major use is not as primary indicators of index levels, but for the visual display of secondary or ancillary indicators, like moving averages, relative strength or open interest.

Point and figure chart

Figure 6.3 is different to Figures 6.1 and 6.2 in that it has no time scale. Price moves are plotted with the horizontal axis showing the occasions that the market changed direction. Crosses indicate an upmove, zeros a downmove. These 'reversals' can be small (i.e. one unit) so in order to cut out too much spurious small movement,

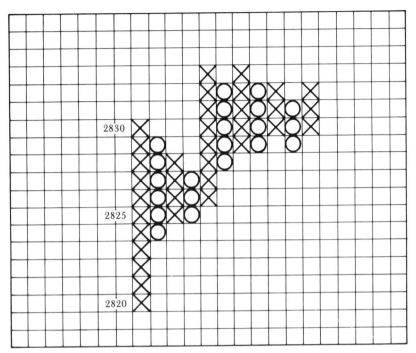

Figure 6.3   Point and figure chart

different traders will choose reversals of different magnitude. The point and figure chart shown in Figure 6.3 uses a minimum three-print reversal, i.e. oscillations within three plotted points are not recorded. The size of the unit of movement or box size can also be adjusted to whatever scale the trader desires. Our example uses unit movements but just as easily these could have been 10-unit moves. Charts of this nature are generally used with a unit scale and are more precise in indicating possible areas of support and resistance on a short-term basis, thus they tend to be the tools of the short-term trader.

Chart scale

Arithmetic scales represent equal amounts for similar underlying values. Over a longer period of time, because of the natural tendency of stock markets to rise to higher and higher levels, using arithmetic scales will cause the more recent moves to go off the top of the page. This can be overcome, and at the same time a different assessment of market movement can be obtained, using logarithmic or semilogarithmic scales. These scales will allow for a percentage comparison to be made between market moves, a 300-point move on an index standing at 3000 would cover the same chart distance as a 200-point move on an index standing at 2000.

Support, resistance and trend channels

Now that we have an awareness that the market may be trending in a particular direction, and we understand the type of squares that we are using in our graph paper, we can start to be more critical of the interpretation of 'the trend'.

Price levels, at which investors believe are the 'correct' levels to either buy equities or the index itself, become known as support areas. A market may come back to a support area several times, but if investors still feel that the level is attractive and at the level at which we have more buyers than sellers, the support will continue to be demonstrated. At higher levels, where investors regularly sell stock and sellers outnumber buyers, the index will find it impossible, at that time, to rise any further and so we have a resistance area. Should the market oscillate several times between these market highs and lows then a trading channel is seen (Figure 6.4). Traders will attempt to buy whenever the market approaches a support area, and sell and also open short positions at the resistance. The channel begins to take on the dimension of a self-controlling market range. Once the trading range is broken there can be quite a sharp movement away from the channel as the more aggressive traders seek to reverse their positions. A new range may be established, higher than the previous range. There will now be natural support at the previous resistance as those traders who did not get out of their short positions when the range was broken on the upside will be hopeful buyers at this level so as to close their losing short positions at close to a break-even level.

As well as this sideways trend that we have just considered, it is more often the case that the channel will slope upwards or downwards, the uptrend exhibiting a series of higher highs and higher lows, while a downtrend shows the converse. No trend, however, lasts forever. There is one popular anti-technical theory that states that once a trend is spotted, it changes! There is also

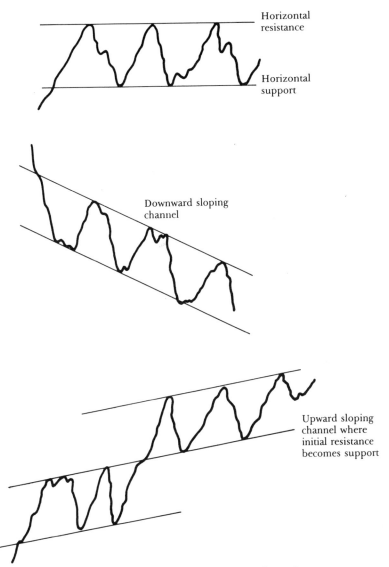

Horizontal
resistance

Horizontal
support

Downward sloping
channel

Upward sloping
channel where
initial resistance
becomes support

Figure 6.4 Support and resistance channels

good statistical evidence that shows that trends will most fre-
quently form three or four points before breaking down, so the best
opportunity that one has for making some rather cunningly timed
trades is to attempt to predict the third point of support or
resistance in a developing channel.

Moving averages

One of the major problems that investors can face is being whiplashed into and out of the market because of uncertainties as to whether a trend is starting to develop or not. Moving averages are used to iron out some of the more volatile short-term movements and can give better buy and sell signals than just by looking at daily high-low and close patterns. Just as earlier we introduced a possible definition of a bull market as one where the index stands above its 200-day moving average, we can extend the definition into a trading signal that we should be going long of the market when the index crosses its moving average in an upward direction. For this purpose the 200-day moving average may only give us signals once or twice a year; consequently, a shorter moving average will exhibit increased volatility and also more buy and sell signals as the index crosses its moving average more times. A 20-day moving average may, therefore, be much more suitable for this purpose.

Why a 20-day moving average and not 15? This question opens a whole area of debate on the suitability of one moving average to another. Regression analysis can be employed to determine which moving average would have given us the best buy and sell signals for any particular stock index (or commodity), but certain conundrums are seen to develop. One moving average may give better buy signals, another better sell signals. One moving average may work very well for a year or more, and then a different one becomes more important. Computer graphics quickly display for us any moving averages we wish to see. From this we can also see that instead of using the index crossing one of its moving averages as a signal, we can instead treat certain moving averages crossing each other as buy or sell signals—a buy signal being when the shorter moving average crosses the longer one, and the converse. Popular moving averages used to give short-term signals are the 5-day and 21-day, representing one trading week and approximately one trading month. The numbers also happen to be those found in the Fibonacci series, and thus of particular significance to certain traders (more of that later). Long-term investors, on the other hand, would use longer periods for their moving averages—possibly a 10-week average and a 30-week average.

As we can see from the chart examples (Figures 6.5 and 6.6),

Figure 6.5 The DAX Index and its 20-day moving average
Source: Datastream plc, 1991. Reproduced with permission

crossing moving averages tend to give fewer signals and fewer periods of uncertainty—when moving averages may or may not cross. The signals do, however, come once the trend is established. A constant problem is that the more certain we wish to be that the trend is correct before committing ourselves, the less profit we will make. If we are equally slow in exiting a changing trend, the net profit on our position may not be as attractive as we might otherwise have hoped.

Instead of a simple arithmetic average, a linear weighted moving average can also be used. This gives more emphasis to the more recent prices. For a 5-day weighted average we would multiply today's price by 5, yesterday's by 4, the day before by 3, etc. The sum of these weightings would then be divided by the total number of 'weights', in this case 15, to give the moving average for that day.

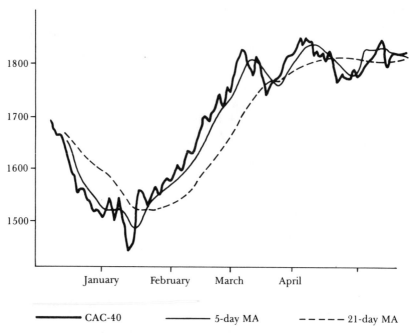

Figure 6.6   CAC-40 with its 5- and 21-day moving averages

Exponentially-weighted average

This is similar in concept to the arithmetically-weighted average in that it also places more importance on more recent data (Figure 6.7). It is calculated by applying a percentage of today's closing price to yesterday's moving average.

With moving averages, it must be remembered that the ideal of being given a buy signal at the bottom of a cycle, and a sell signal at the top, is impossible. Our data, although historic, is attempting to show a change of trend as it happens, but with the elimination of most false starts. It is yet another discipline that will ensure that once a major trend does start, we will be on the right side of it.

Even though the number of buy or sell signals that moving averages give is fewer than a simple trend-following strategy, periods of limited market movement will still result in a considerable number of false starts. Figure 6.6 shows a very good 'buy' signal on the CAC-40 in January; this buy signal caught a 250-point move before it was negated. Subsequently, the market

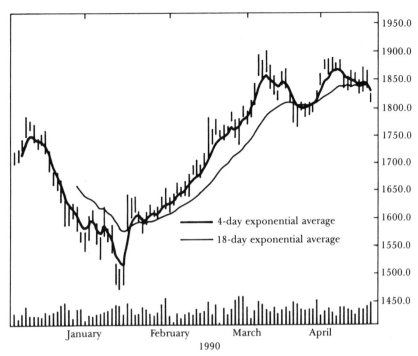

Figure 6.7 CAC-40 future
Source: Market Directional Analysts Ltd, 1991. Reproduced with
permission

entered a period of consolidation and as a result 'buy' and 'sell'
signals did not give good results.

In an attempt to reduce these false starts as far as possible other
more complex considerations can be used.

The MACD

This is short for the 'moving average convergence divergence'
indicator, and it is a moving average modification that seeks to
eliminate some of the false signals that we get from simple moving
averages. It is calculated by subtracting the exponential moving
average of a longer period from the exponential moving average of
a shorter period, the shorter period being about half that of the
longer. Typical periods used would be 26 days and 12 days, or 20
days and 10 days.

These indicators are then plotted together with a shorter expo-

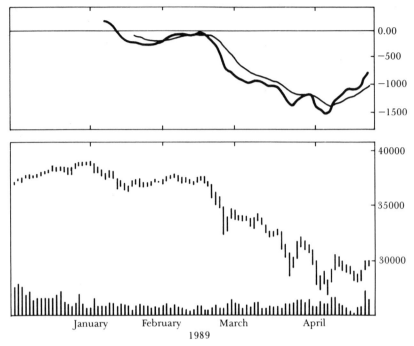

Figure 6.8 Nikkei Index and MACD
Source: Market Directional Analysts Ltd, 1990. Reproduced with
permission

nential moving average, usually 9 days, which is used as the trigger
line for trading signals. When the MACD rises above the trigger
line we have a buy signal, or a sell signal for the converse.

The MACD gives good signals for an intermediate trend, and
gives fewer false starts than simple moving averages. However, as
with all moving average based indicators, if the market stubbornly
refuses to develop a trend we may still be triggered into or out of
the market with monotonous and costly regularity. The more
certain that we wish to be of the validity of a particular trend, the
less potential profit it has remaining.

Figure 6.8 shows the Nikkei Index with its 26/12-day MACD
and 9-day trigger. The long downward trend has been captured,
but periods of uncertainty still give some false signals.

Volume and open interest

Changes in trading volume and the open interest can give confir-
mations that a particular trend is gathering momentum, often
before our chosen moving averages give us a trading signal. The
generally accepted view is that an increase in trading volume
confirms the particular trend that is underway. A price rise on
increased volume shows increased participation which should
sustain the move. A price rise on decreasing volume indicates
decreasing participation and an index level that is becoming
vulnerable to a setback. Conversely, increasing volume with declining prices confirms the downtrend. As well as a straightforward
look at daily trading volumes to give us an impression of how
volume is changing, we can construct moving averages of daily
volumes to give us a better impression without the 'interference' of
short-term volatility. Some analysts prefer to use volumes of
equities traded in the underlying index rather than the number of
futures contracts. While the number of equities traded should be
reflected in the degree of interest in the futures market, it can be
useful to determine whether for a particular equity market one is a
better indicator of changing trends than the other.

Open interest gives similar confirmation to market moves as
does trading volume. The published figures for open interest are
for one side only, i.e. an open interest of one means that there is
one long and one short in the market (shrewder traders may have
noticed that occasionally open interest does end in an odd
number—impossible if one purchase and one sale resulted in an
open interest of two!). As with trading volume, rising open interest
indicates that the established trend will continue. In a rising
market the open interest will continue to increase while the short
holders are prepared to run their losses and the longs are not yet
ready to take profits. When this does start to happen the trend will
begin to weaken. No new players will come to sustain the upward
push, with the outcome that the index may start to fall back.

Similarly in a bear market, while open interest is rising bear
traders can feel comfortable that downward momentum is being
maintained. When open interest starts to fall we may be approach-
ing a near-term bottom.

The different emphasis that volume and open interest may show
is that increasing volume tends to be a better indicator of the start

of a trend, declining open interest possibly a better indicator that a trend may be running out of momentum.

Summary of volume and open interest indications
1. During a major uptrend, volume tends to increase on rallies but decline on setbacks.
2. In a major downtrend, volume tends to increase as the market continues down but decreases on rallies.
3. Large increases in volume may be seen as tops or bottoms are neared.
4. If open interest increases as the market rises or falls the established market trend is well supported.
5. If open interest decreases as the market rises or falls then the established trend can be regarded as weak.
6. An important top or bottom (often known as a blow-off top or bottom) is often associated with a sharp increase in volume but a heavy fall in open interest.

Chart patterns

The sceptics who decry technical analysis *per se* are usually those who have come across the technical interpretation of a chart pattern, and found it unconvincing. The rest of the 'science' is then written off into the same lunatic pigeonhole. This is a shame, because it can be argued that although the 'chart-pattern' aspect of technical analysis is the popular face of the subject, it is one of the least important. To give some credit to the sceptic, there seems little logical reason as to *why* any chart pattern should work. The argument that a double bottom or flag formation is a graphical representation of mass psychology is tempting, but on uncertain ground if all the trading masses (or even a significant section) are aware of the pattern. A self-fulfilling prophecy can rapidly degenerate into a game of pass-the-parcel or musical chairs.

Nevertheless, a point in favour of chart patterns is that they are relatively few in number and have remained unchanged since the turn of the century when they were first developed. For these reasons alone it is worth being aware of them; had they been totally spurious they would have been abandoned a long time ago. It is also worth spelling out just what these patterns seek to indicate. We are looking for a signal that a trend may change, may pause or develop strongly—all of these being possibly given additional confirmation through a consideration of volumes, open interest, moving averages as well as other technical tools.

Double or triple tops or bottoms

In a way, double or triple tops or bottoms are similar to the major points on a sideways channel, but seen as a very much larger formation over a longer period. They are seen where the market makes similar high or low levels two or three times. Investors may see this as an indication that a particular low or high cannot currently be broken and, therefore, the trend may be changing. A move through the fulcrum of a double top or bottom is often seen as confirmation that a particular double top or bottom has checked the old trend. A double or triple bottom should thus be regarded as a good buying opportunity, a double or triple top as a good level at which to go short.

Head and shoulders tops and bottoms

A head and shoulders top is so called because the chart pattern is supposed to look like the front profile of a person (Figure 6.9). This is a major top formation where the major high (the head) is sandwiched between two lower, approximately symmetrical peaks (the shoulders). A major top gives a sell signal when the market breaks the neckline after completing the second shoulder. The projected decline that is then expected is similar to that already seen from the peak to the neckline. Conversely, a major area of support and, therefore, a change of trend from down to up may be indicated by a reversed head and shoulders pattern. Analysts will also use the slope of the neckline as additional confirmation that the overall trend may be changing. A head and shoulders top should have a downward sloping neckline, in part similar in indication to a downward trending channel where we see lower and lower tops and bottoms.

Flags and triangles

A triangle is occasionally seen when the market momentarily enters a period of decreasing volatility exhibited by lower highs

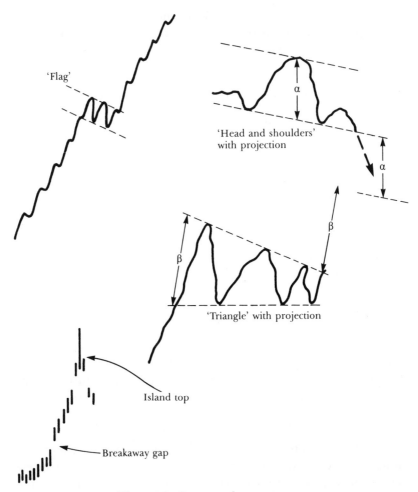

Figure 6.9 Common chart patterns

and higher lows (Figure 6.9). The market usually reasserts the
original trend with a break out of the formation before the apex of
the triangle is reached. A period such as this will represent a period
of consolidation by the market. Once the market breaks out of the
triangle a target level for the market to reach is exhibited and is
equal to the length of the first formed side of the triangle. A flag is
a similar period of consolidation within a strong trend but, instead
of being triangular, is seen as a short channel sloping in the
opposite direction to the main trend. Once the main trend resumes,
technicians will be looking for the resumed trend to be of equivalent

dimension to that seen before the flag, in other words, for the purposes of technical analysis, a flag always flies at half-mast.

Gaps

Several varieties of 'gap' are recognized, but they are all formed when one day's trading movement does not overlap the range of the previous day. This may be caused by the market opening sharply higher or lower than the previous day's close as a result of important overnight news, strong movements in overseas markets influencing our market of interest, or quite simply because the market has started to develop a strong momentum of its own.

The first variety of gap that is seen is the 'breakaway gap'. This usually occurs soon after a new trend has been established as large numbers of new investors suddenly want to join the action. It is often regarded as a confirmation that the new trend is well established.

During a particular run in the market a 'runaway' gap can also occur. Often this will be the method by which the market conspires to break through established resistance or support areas. It is regarded similarly to a flag formation in that it may signify the half-way point to an existing trend, confirming that the market still has the momentum to push further in the same direction.

Finally, there may be an 'exhaustion' gap at the end of a particular trend, often seen in conjunction with an increase in trading volume and a decrease in open interest to confirm that the trend is indeed over. An extension of the exhaustion gap is the 'island reversal'. This indicates that not only is the existing trend over, but a new opposite trend may be starting. It is equivalent to a joined exhaustion and breakaway gap; it can be a single-day phenomenon or the island can be of a few days' duration.

The gap represents an area where no trading was done, and thus a range of prices where no contracts were made. It is often observed that at a later stage the market will attempt to fill its gaps. This may be so, but the timing for this is indeterminate—it may take months sometimes for gaps to be filled. What is worth noting is that when being filled, the far side of the gap may become a temporary resistance (or support) area.

Climaxes or blow offs

Climaxes or blow offs can be regarded in the same light as exhaustion gaps, except that there is no gap! Instead we see a very large trading range that lasts just one or two days, after which the market starts to reverse the old trend.

Key reversals and reversal days

Key reversals and reversal days are minor trend change indicators to be used even more as 'just a guide' to possible new directions of the market than the other chart patterns. A key reversal is a new high or low that exhibits 'weakness' in that although during the day the market made new highs (or lows), the close was below the close of the previous day (or above in the case of a key reversal in a reversing downtrend). It should also be accompanied by higher volume than on previous days, and as it has arisen as a result of profit taking, a drop in open interest should also be seen in due course.

A reversal day is similar to a key reversal except that it does not make a new trading high or low for the trend, it just exhibits the 'weak close'. Consequently, it is not as strong a signal as the key reversal—which in any case should be regarded as a less reliable signal than many of those that we have considered earlier.

Rounded tops and saucer bottoms

As the names suggest these are gently curved top or bottom patterns. In a saucer bottom, declining prices slowly level off before rising gently with an accompanied increase in trading volume. Volumes, however, generally for these formations are low.

Oscillators

A whole range of technical indicators that are based on measuring changes in index levels, rather than the absolute levels, are given the term 'oscillators'. The variety of oscillators used is constantly being widened and refined, and their calculation can be very complex. We shall look at just the main generic types (Figures 6.10–6.12).

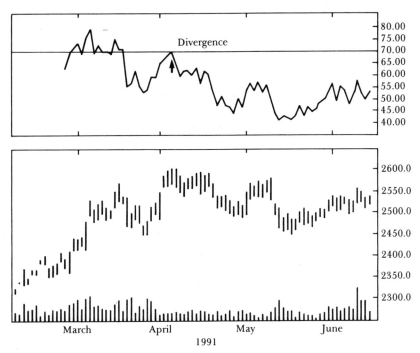

Figure 6.10   FT-SE June 1991 and 14 RSI
Source: Market Directional Analysts Ltd, 1991.
Reproduced with permission

The relative strength index (RSI)

This is an oscillator that ranges between 0 and 100 (Figure 6.10).
It is calculated with the formula:

$$RSI = 100 \times \left(\frac{U}{U + D} \right)$$

U is an average over a defined number of days of the upward price
changes; D is the similar average of downward price changes.
Popular periods are 9 or 10 days. A historic RSI can then be
investigated to find between which levels the index resides for most
of the time. Generally, an RSI above 70 indicates an overbought
market; below 30, oversold. In simpler language this means that
the market has reached particular high or low levels so quickly
that there needs to be a period of consolidation before the market
can again be regarded as 'stable'. Thus an overbought market

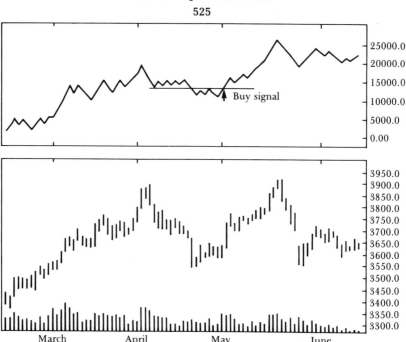

Figure 6.11 Hang Seng cash and OBV
Source: Market Directional Analysts Ltd, 1991.
Reproduced with permission

would need some sort of setback, or possibly a period of stability before a new upward thrust could be envisaged. It is also possible that resistance to further upward movement in the market is seen firstly in the RSI, and only subsequently in the index level itself. The RSI is a particularly interesting indicator if it is failing to confirm the trend of the underlying market. Under these circumstances it is an early warning that the existing market trend has lost all momentum and is likely to reverse.

On balance volume

This oscillator is a combination of price and volume. It is calculated by adding the last day's traded volume to a cumulative total when the market closes higher, but subtracting the day's volume when the market closes lower. This technique seeks to identify large movements of money into or out of the market, the theory being that if many large volume players enter the market, the market will respond and move accordingly. This to a certain degree infers that the market will respond after large volume players have entered the market and, as a result, this indicator is often regarded as a leading signal to probable market direction rather than a confirmatory, or lagging indicator.

Momentum

This is also known as the 'rate of change indicator' and seeks to quantify the well recognized phenomenon that the market will sometimes surge forward (or downwards) over a period of time, and at other times move very gently. Momentum indicators show this market movement as a wave oscillation. The faster that the market rises or falls, the faster will the momentum rise. In a quiet market, momentum will be neutral.

Momentum is calculated by dividing the price change over the last 'n' days by the closing level of the market 'n' days ago. This gives us a percentage figure representing how the market's level has changed in the last 'n' days, or its momentum. A very short period of just one or two days will give a very erratic chart pattern, not really of much use in trying to assess whether a trend is slowing down. A long period of a year or more is interesting to analyse for identification of long-term cycles. Most investment analysts would, however, use 5-day, 10-day or 20-day periods as these give the best indications for the more popular investment trades, or timing for longer term investments.

The momentum percentage can be made negative for downward movements in the market so as to give a true oscillation pattern between −100 per cent and +100 per cent. This will give us a pattern like the RSI where by experience we can define a particular market to be either overbought or oversold. A 10-day momentum indicator tends to oscillate with a fair but not excessive degree of movement for most stock index markets and some market movements can be anticipated from considerations of previous patterns and their relationship to the movements of the underlying market.

Stochastic oscillators

Stochastic oscillators are a little more complex in both calculation and interpretation (Figure 6.12). This oscillator seeks to show

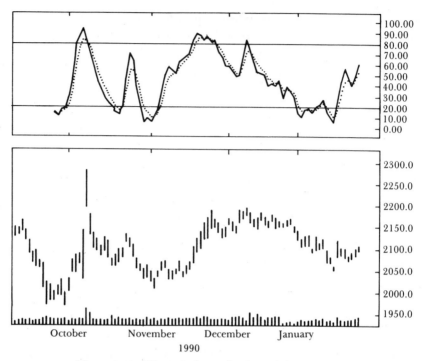

Figure 6.12   FT 100 Index and 9% K 3% D stochastic
Source: Market Directional Analysts Ltd, 1991.
Reproduced with permission

where the market closed relative to its trading range over a defined
number of days. The oscillator will range between 0 per cent and
100 per cent, a level of 0 per cent indicating that the market's close
today was the lowest level for the market during the period that
the oscillator is calculated, a level of 100 per cent indicating the
highest level for the period. The formula for calculating the
stochastic oscillator for a period of 'n' days is:

$$\frac{\text{today's close—lowest close in 'n' days}}{\text{highest high in 'n' days—lowest low in 'n' days}}$$

The general observation that stochastic oscillators seek to quantify
is that as the market rises, closing prices will tend towards the
highs of the day, and the calculated period; in a declining market,
continuing weakness will be demonstrated by closing prices being
nearer the lows of the calculated period. If the closing levels are no
longer 'pushing' the market in a particular direction then the trend

may be coming to an end. A stochastic oscillator is often used in conjunction with its own moving average, with the two indicators crossing to give a confirmatory change of trend signal. It can also be viewed in the same way as other overbought/oversold indicators in that when the stochastic oscillator is above or below an historically significant level the trend of the market may be becoming unsustainable, and a reverse is indicated. Often a market will remain in overbought or oversold territory for some time. A safer signal may be obtained as the indicator reverses across its overbought oversold lines.

Technical traps

This list by no means seeks to exhaust all possible oscillators as well as other indicators that investment analysts use. Indeed, new indicators are constantly being sought and analysts or traders will gravitate from one to another as they feel that better signals in a particular market are obtained *for them* by a specific oscillator. Unfortunately, with increased sophistication it is all too easy to lose sight of one's original objectives—to make money. A highly skilled technician can develop oscillators of infinite complexity, which then insulate him from having to take any trading decisions, relying instead on buy or sell signals from the mathematical model. One's trading discipline is housed in mathematical formulae. It can work, profits can be generated, but the cost may be loss of that enigmatic property—market feel. Just as with chart patterns or the assessment of trends it is worth remembering that all these indicators will continue to work—until they don't.

While it may be overstating the obvious that if all traders used the same technical indicators they would cease to have any value, it is as well to avoid following any technical indicator blindly. Any self-fulfilling technical prophecy has the potential of becoming a technical trap. The average institutional investor will (we hope) regard with great suspicion any claim that it is possible to 'work-a-system' at the races, roulette or a lottery. One sometimes wonders whether a more sophisticated mind is not beguiled by intellectual complexity into believing that technical analysis may be the philosophers' stone of investment.

If we abandon any urges that we may have in developing a totally mechanical investment system, there are nevertheless many important factors in technical analysis that any investor can use with advantage.

Firstly, technical analysis is yet another form of discipline—the discipline to look for trends, to look for patterns, to consider market indicators and to be aware that they may all change. Secondly, by following a disciplined approach to trading and considering various technical aspects, we are constantly gaining information about the market and thus improving our own judgement on the timing of trades. Possibly the greatest conundrum of technical analysis is that it can help the development of 'market feel'. The quantification of the successful 'seat-of-the-pants-approach'—the psychology behind the hunch.

Japanese candlesticks

Although 'traditional' western technical analysis traces its roots back only to the turn of this century, many of the patterns used as trading guides have been identified many centuries earlier. Japanese candlestick charts (Figures 6.13–6.15), so called because trading information is displayed by what appear to be candles with a wick at each end, are traced back to the early seventeenth century where they were used to improve trading decisions in the rice markets.

Similar in concept to bar charts they do, however, give an improved visual impression of market activity. Opening, closing and the day's high and low points are plotted. The body of the 'candle' is drawn between the opening and closing level, and coloured black if the close is below the opening (a down day), and left white if the close is higher than the opening price (an up day). This gives rise to the following possible candlestick shapes (see p. 133).

A period when the market is exhibiting higher and higher prices will comprise mainly white candles. Warnings that the market may be ending its upward rush will be given by black candles, and a bear market will have a far greater share of black than white candles. Specific signals or warnings of a possible change of trend are given some rather exotic names, and in many of these patterns can be seen similarities to concepts such as 'reversal days', 'island tops' and 'gaps'. Some of the major candlestick patterns are given below.

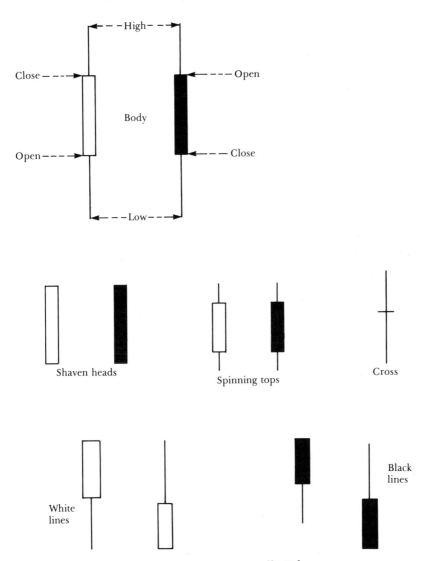

Figure 6.13 Japanese candlesticks

Piercing line or sunny sky   Here a white candle closes more than half way above the body of the previous day's black candle, indicating the possible start of an upward trend.

Dark clouds   A hint of bad times to come. The opposite of sunny sky, similar to a key reversal where the second day's black body closes below the previous day's white body half-way line.

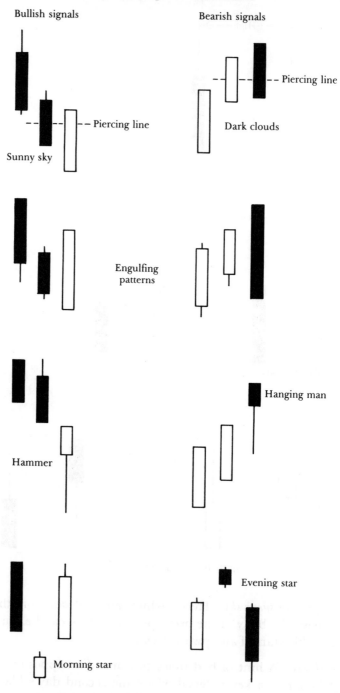

Figure 6.14 Bullish and bearish signals

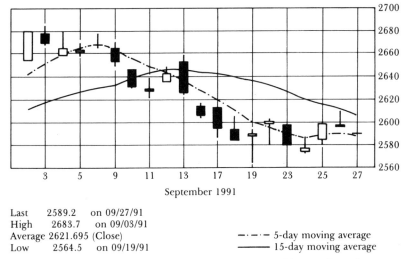

Last	2589.2 on 09/27/91
High	2683.7 on 09/03/91
Average	2621.695 (Close)
Low	2564.5 on 09/19/91

— · — 5-day moving average
———— 15-day moving average

Figure 6.15   FT-SE 100 Index chart as represented by candlesticks
Source: Bloomberg plc, 1991. Reproduced with permission

Engulfing patterns These become significant after a prolonged market move when the second day's shadowless (wickless) body engulfs that of the previous day. They are bullish where the second day's candle is white, bearish when black.

Morning star and evening star A small candle that has 'gapped' away from a trend of larger candles. These are trend reversal indicators.

Hanging man or hammer Similar formations with the hanging man indicating a top, the hammer indicating a bottom. In each case the colour of the candle is not relevant.

Contrary opinion

'Contrary opinion' is a slightly oddball semi-technical consideration that has as its underlying premiss the concept that the majority is usually wrong. At first glance this appears to fly in the face of any thoughts that we should try to spot a trend as early as possible, and then run with the trend for as long as possible. However, this is not quite so. As a trend starts, only a few investors are convinced that it is a trend—they will hold long positions, other investors will be short or undecided. Once the trend becomes more established, more will join in. Finally, in an ideal situation, all the remaining bears will change their minds and become bulls, and so everyone will be convinced that the market is going up. As it is only natural to talk one's book, the fact that everyone is now convinced the market will continue its trend also implies that everyone is long and, therefore, there is no one left to do any more buying. The contrarian will at this point be the first to anticipate a change of market direction.

Unfortunately, there is great difficulty in determining what all the other investors are thinking. Newspapers occasionally will carry out surveys, as will other private services, canvassing opinion just as in a political opinion poll. If the result of such a survey finds 70 per cent of institutional investors 'bullish', one could argue that the bullish consensus is still not high enough to warrant shorting the market on the basis of 'contrary opinion'. If it were possible to 'capitalization weight' these institutional investors by the volume of funds under their management, we might find that 85 per cent were in the bullish consensus school. This level can be considered to be far closer to the 'overbought level' than 70 per cent, so while we may not regard this as a definite sell signal it can be used as a warning sign that the market is apparently running out of significant buyers.

Any statistical interpretation of contrary opinion, as the foregoing shows, can be very suspect. It would also be wrong to regard a contrarian as someone who merely wishes to stand against the crowd just for the sheer devilry of it. For a valid contrarian view, two or possibly three factors should be seen in the market:

1. The expected forward direction of the market must be virtually taken for granted. Everyone will be talking the market down to a particular level, or up to a particular level. It may even be that the market has started to trade in a very narrow range and universal opinion decrees that the market will not move 'at least for two more months'. All these are circumstances where the contrarian can start to look for trading opportunities.
2. The reasons that are used to support the popular view are no longer as powerful as they were originally—and may actually no longer be valid at all. It is, however, comforting to repeat, without the need for original thought, something that everyone else has been saying for some time. Under such circumstances, unpleasant facts, or information that does not confirm the

accepted view, are not paid the required degree of attention. Misplaced faith makes unpleasant facts invisible.

3. The bubble effect. Just occasionally this particular phenomenon of mass psychology rears its head. A particular trend starts, is established, draws in more and more players none of whom wish to miss out on the best investment opportunity of their lifetimes and the price explodes, defying both gravity and logic. Popular reasons are given as to why the price must continue to rise, generally because a so-called major re-evaluation of fundamentals is taking place. In the late stages of a 'bubble' investors are still scrambling to get in, and even some who suspect that the investment may not be all that good, often believe that they can get out quickly if the market starts to look tired. Under such circumstances, it takes a very brave investor to hold the contrary view, but equally it is this contrary view that ultimately is the pin that bursts the bubble. The contrarian may well turn out to be the only investor who managed to take a profit on what may, subsequently, become an unsaleable stock or a market that then needs three years to recover. Unlike many other technical forms of analysis, contrary opinion does not seek to provide, buy or sell signals. It is an approach that seeks to question what is going on and why. Any market situation where strong unidirectional opinions are held, makes for an anomalous market. Contrary opinion seeks to identify and take advantage of the situation when strong opinions are still driving a market, but the underlying reasons for the opinions are no longer in evidence.

Other exotica

It is not within the scope of this book to analyse the more obscure forms of technical analysis, many of which, like the 'gurus' that promote them, work well for a period before failing and then disappearing. Three names, however, have endured over the years; Fibonacci, Elliot and Gann; and while a purely fundamental investor will find some of the ideas associated with these three names rather strange, they nevertheless have a substantial following. The notes that follow are of necessity brief, and so those interested in exploring these subjects further should refer to the bibliography.

Fibonacci

Leonardo Fibonacci, a Florentine mathematician living in the twelfth and thirteenth centuries, is credited with the development of an infinite series or sequence of numbers in which each number (a Fibonacci number) is the sum of the previous two, i.e. 0, 1, 1, 2, 3, 5, 8, etc. Although Fibonacci 'discovered' the sequence while investigating the growth in population of breeding pairs of rabbits, the series has subsequently been seen in many aspects of nature and physics. There is no magic about these numbers, they merely represent a simple growth system that is also seen in natural phenomena.

Fibonacci ratios are obtained by dividing a Fibonacci number by the number preceding it. This gives a ratio of approximately 1.618 and an inverse of 0.618, divergence from these ratios being greater for the earlier values in the sequence than for later ones. The ratio of 1.618 is also referred to as the Golden Number, and like the Fibonacci series, also crops up as a ratio in many natural phenomena. Of specific interest to investors is the fact that both the series and the ratios can be seen to occur in various aspects of the financial markets, the ratios indicating possible differentials between significant market highs and lows, the numbers them- selves representing time periods when important trend changes may occur. Aficionados interpret this as natural laws affecting crowd behaviour—this may well be the case even though at this stage research on the subject is inconclusive. Perhaps that is an attraction. If markets were 'proved' to respond in line with Fibonacci's series and ratios and we all attempted to trade accordingly, it would not work!

R. N. Elliott and his waves

After retiring as an accountant, and having spent a great deal of time analysing stock market movements, in 1938 Elliott published his theories of the wave principle. This wave theory has as its underlying tenet the observation that a bull market will exhibit a five-wave advance, followed by a three-wave decline. Each com- plete cycle has thus eight waves. Impulse waves move in the direction of the main trend, corrective waves against it. Each wave can, however, be divided into smaller waves, and each main wave exhibits its own peculiarities, i.e. wave three being the longest and most dynamic. The relationship between the heights of succeeding waves are calculated using Fibonacci ratios and time targets are determined by Fibonacci days, i.e. 8, 13 or 21 days forward.

The Elliott wave theory does have a substantial following in investment circles, even though it is often easier to spot the wave patterns after the event rather than as they happen. The case really is not proven either way. Certainly, it is possible that a positively developing market will exhibit similar characteristics to a similar bull market that occurred at some earlier period of time—just as a lone walker climbing a mountain may stumble or pause for breath at exactly the same points as have hundreds of other climbers over the centuries. The sceptics may point to the fact that as it is impossible in every case to define a 'wave', the theory is far too flexible in that using the same data different analysts can arrive at different interpretations on likely market outcomes. Also Elliott's later attempts to tie his wave theory to the mathematical relation-ships of the great pyramid at Gizeh, and so predict future world events, was not helpful.

W. D. Gann

Gann is probably one of the most enigmatic of investors. Many so-called 'gurus' explain their particular methods (or disciplines!) for making good returns in the markets. Gann was rather different in that he actually made vast amounts of money from investing in various markets, but never revealed exactly how this was achieved. His published works confirm the need for trading discipline, the need to recognize short-, medium- and long-term trends. He advocated the use of stops to protect capital and recognized that support or resistance levels would be at certain ratios to previous highs and lows. Gann also used circles and angles drawn from significant highs or lows to indicate possible future times when significant trend changes could be expected.

Students of Gann often complain that there appears to be so much to remember when attempting to trade following Gann's ideas, that one is often overwhelmed and reduced to inactivity. Certainly, Gann did leave a lot of clear disciplines that are relevant to any trader. Many of his ideas, based on his own research, are very complex, but the exact and detailed calculations that he made which time and time again, on many well-documented occasions, allowed him to buy at the bottom and sell at the top, often during intra-day moves, were never revealed.

It is not difficult to imagine why. The moment that any such technique is revealed to the market is the same moment that it ceases to be effective. Why, therefore, destroy both the income and the mystery.

Gann was a great advocate of personal research. With so many markets to choose from, where over a period of time many traders become set in their ways, it is not beyond the bounds of reasonable expectation that with diligence one may spot patterns that under similar circumstances will be seen to repeat themselves. A group of human beings are, after all, much more predictable under most sets of circumstances than a perfectly engineered roulette wheel.

CHAPTER 7

Fundamental factors affecting stock indices

The hard core of technical traders will wish to have nothing at all to do with fundamental market considerations, believing that they serve only to confuse the mind with an endless stream of often conflicting economic data. Nevertheless, it is market fundamentals that are the driving forces in index movements, and while the variety and number of economic or systematic risk factors that can be considered is vast, only about a dozen or so are generally regarded as of major importance.

Economic statistics in themselves are far less important than the market expectation for them. An expected very bad economic statistic that turns out to be only mildly disastrous can cause a substantial market rally. When the market is in the grip of strong bullish sentiment, bad economic figures cause either a short lived reaction or none at all; good figures, on the other hand, cause the market to leap even higher. The reverse, of course, is a bear phase. One economic statistic, therefore, is not the governor of the trend, it is just one part of the overall tapestry. However, several bad economic statistics may prompt investors into thinking that a bullish trend is changing.

It is also apparent that some economic statistics are regarded as very important, others less so, but this relative importance is not constant and changes as if following the vagaries of fashion. This may be true to a degree, but the argument that the perceived importance of an economic statistic is relative to its significance in the economic cycle is sounder.

Business cycles in a nutshell

All economic activity oscillates between periods of high and low activity. Different researchers have identified economic cycles that can be traced back into history, different products being affected by differing main cycles, and also being affected by the peaks or troughs of other influencing cycles. Stock markets are an integral part of the business cycle so in order to assess fundamental influences we have to know where in the business cycle we find ourselves.

As a business cycle starts, with increasing activity we see wages climbing and unemployment reducing as workforces are expanded to capture increasing demand for goods brought about by greater spending power. Increased demand means that even more capacity is then created to prepare for the further projected increases that business expects. Profits grow, expectations of profits grow, share prices climb steadily to reflect increasing dividends, and wages increase. At the top of the cycle, just when everything is going like a dream, orders start to fall off (everyone else has been increasing capacity too), profit margins come under pressure, and high interest rates, pulled up by an increasing borrowing demand, refuse to decline and eat further into profit margins. Unproductive overcapacity becomes a financial millstone. Sections of industry become redundant, unemployment rises. Wages no longer attempt to exceed inflation. Spending on luxury items falls faster than on other items. Interest rates may start to drop. Prices in certain areas certainly do. Dividends are reduced. Equities and stock indices are already sinking to lows. At cycle lows, bad economic news piles up on yet more bad economic news and is often associated with bad political news as well.

Inevitably, before the cycle turns the economy appears so bad that many economists start to make further projections about just how much worse things are likely to become. Then, often imperceptibly the mood changes, either because of a cut in interest rates, an increase in orders or because of the feeling that sooner or later demand will pick up; and so the cycle is underway again, often with the equity market leading the way. Because of the interrelation between international investments, an improving cycle in one country can quickly affect others as well. Whereas for many years after the war the American economy was regarded as being so big

Figure 7.1   FT-SE 100 Index over 10 years
Source: Datastream plc, 1991. Reproduced with permission

that it was the driving force of the economic world, with the advent of the Japanese economy and now the integration of European economies, this is no longer an automatic assumption. The three economic blocks, while to some degree interdependent, are nevertheless powerful in their own rights and are now less likely to be affected by each other's problems than previously.

Although in business cycles we can see cycles of increasing and then decreasing activity, increasing and decreasing interest rates, a chart showing equity prices over a long period indicates that times of actual recession are very few (Figure 7.1). Business cycles in the main indicate periodic slowdowns in an economy's rate of growth.

As a business cycle is made up of every aspect of economic activity, all economic pointers are carefully monitored to determine how stockmarket prices will be affected. It is to these many aspects that we now turn.

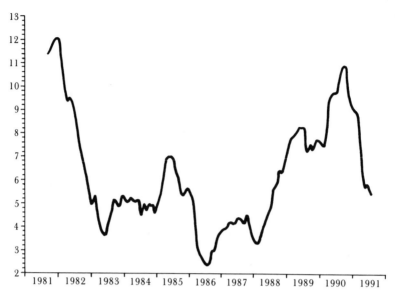

Figure 7.2   Retail Price Index over 10 years
Source: Datastream plc, 1991. Reproduced with permission

Inflation indicators

Retail prices   A 'basket' of retail goods is monitored for the purpose of assessing retail price inflation (Figure 7.2). Increasing inflation suggests higher interest rates, a weakening currency, and an excess of money chasing too few goods. In the short term, increased retail prices tend to have a negative effect on equity prices—in the longer term the effect is less severe as equity prices, the same as all prices, have to rise to reflect inflationary forces. This does not, however, reflect any increase in value.

Average earnings   These have to be monitored with regard to retail prices (Figure 7.3). A high figure for earnings may be an indicator that the economy is growing strongly and can afford to pay increased wages. In the latter stages of the cycle, wages that are still higher than retail prices will be a contributory factor in decreasing corporate profitability. Average earnings figures tend to have more impact on equity prices at times when wage rounds start to be negotiated. Once a trend for wages has been established their importance diminishes.

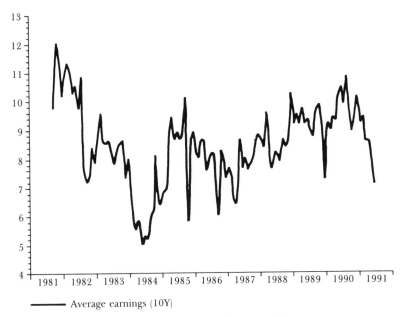

Figure 7.3 Average earnings over 10 years
Source: Datastream plc, 1991. Reproduced with permission

Activity indicators

Manufacturing production Increasing volume of goods produced confirms an upward trend in the economic cycle and is bullish for equities so long as this is not associated with stock building, i.e. production but no consumption. Decreasing manufacturing production is a sign that activity is slowing down and profits are being reduced.

Unemployment Low unemployment is characteristic of an upswing in the business cycle as employers seek to increase production to meet the demand for goods and services. Increasing unemployment then followed by increasing employment tends to be very much cyclical following behind the business cycle as a lagging indicator. It is of more use in confirming other trends than giving a hint of the way the economy is developing (Figure 7.4).

Balance of payments The balance of payments is made up of visible and invisible payments, and gauges the performance of the UK against the rest of the world (Figure 7.5). It is the difference between

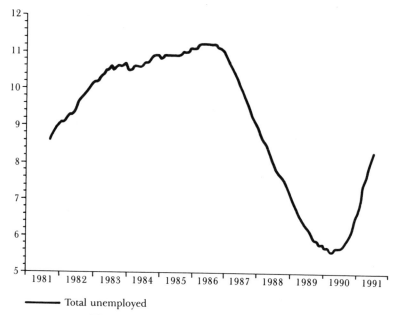

Figure 7.4 Unemployment over 10 years
Source: Datastream plc, 1991. Reproduced with permission

the value of exported goods and services plus inflows from the invisibles like interest, profits, dividends, and the value of imported goods and services together with outflows on other invisibles. The balance of payments is, therefore, unlikely ever to be in balance. If the balance is a surplus then there is pressure for this to be invested abroad; if the balance is in deficit it has to be financed either from foreign borrowing or the utilization of official reserves.

Since the end of the Britton Woods fixed exchange rate agreement in 1972, trade figures have been closely monitored for signs that the exchange rate will be affected. A weakening currency as a result of a negative balance of payments, therefore, may require higher interest rates for its support, and this in turn becomes bearish for equities. Since the advent of stirling joining the European Monetary System, similarities with the old Bretton Woods agreements emerge, interest rates having become a more direct weapon with which to stabilize currencies.

In retrospect, changes in the balance of trade become clear and easy to comprehend. The published monthly figures are often confusing, prone to revision (often substantial) and subject to

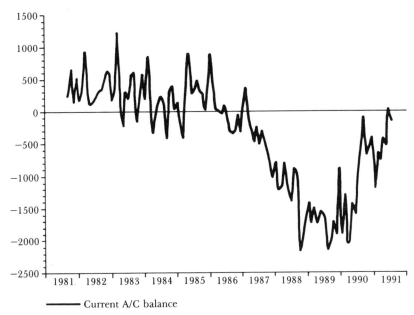

Figure 7.5 Balance of payments over 10 years
Source: Datastream plc, 1991. Reproduced with permission

considerable distortions. Large capital items such as aircraft, ships and precious stones are itemized, but nevertheless still form part of the import-export balance. Statistical allowance is made for annual fluctuations and numbers of working days in the month.

In essence, a positive trade balance is good news for the equity market, but the information published, while likely to have a significant short-term market impact if actual figures turn out to be out-of-line with those expected, must be regarded with suspicion. 'Final' revised figures showing a definite trend are more significant and important to the long-term investor.

Financial indicators

PSBR

The public sector borrowing requirement represents the extra money needed to support the public sector, and is financed by the issue of gilt-edged stock (Figure 7.6). The size of the PSBR is a guide to the financial efficiency with which the government is

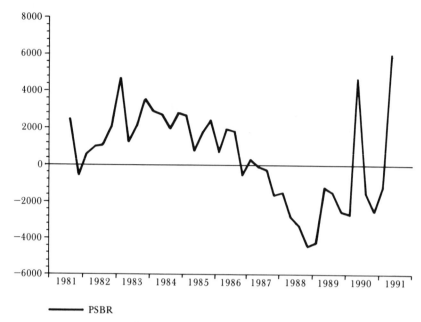

Figure 7.6   PSBR over 10 years
Source: Datastream plc, 1991. Reproduced with permission

working, and hence an indicator on short-term interest rates. If the government needs to borrow a lot of money, then interest rates are likely to rise, which in turn is bad for the equity market.

Over the last few years there has been a move by the government to reduce the PSBR; during the late 1980s a PSDR or public sector debt repayment became the order of the day. This has resulted in the PSBR becoming less important as an indicator on short-term interest rates, than exchange rates.

The reduction of the PSBR (or overseas equivalent) has now become a more fashionable international aim, basically achieved by improved economic housekeeping, aided to some degree by the privatization of government assets.

Monetary indicators

These are given the rather unromantic titles of MO, M1, M2, M3, M4 and M5. Often they are not regarded as particularly important. Only when one or other is seen to be getting out of control, and an indication is given that, for instance, credit is rising too rapidly, can short-term or long-term changes in interest rates be expected, with the expected effect on equities.

MO   This represents the actual notes and coins in circulation, and, contrary to popular opinion, is not very easy to control. Switching off the printing presses might cause scarcity, but also a run on the banks. In any event, with the development of more forms of cashless trading MO is slowly losing its significance.

M1   This is an older definition than MO although it is similar. M1 comprises the notes and coins in circulation, as MO, but also includes bank deposits. Initially, the bank deposits used in calculating M1 were those that could be promptly withdrawn but on which no interest was paid, such as current accounts. However, large overnight deposits on which interest was paid were included, and more recently as banks have started to pay interest on current accounts the original definition has become outdated. Also, because of the changing environment, i.e. banks starting to pay interest on promptly withdrawable cash, M1 has shown a considerable increase—but not because of any real increase in the money supply, only because of an erosion to the original definition, a neat example of the sort of problem that any definition of money supply encounters sooner or later.

M2   This is made up of coins and notes in circulation, non-interest bearing short-term bank deposits plus all other deposits of less than £100 000 with less than one month's notice of withdrawal. It includes building society deposits that fall into the definition.

M3   This consists of M1 plus all deposits in banks and discount houses. M3 is sometimes used by governments as a target figure for the control of money supply—it can only be used as a guide to how government policy is proceeding. M3 does not include foreign currency deposits.

M4   M3 plus building society deposits.

M5   M4 plus National Savings and money market instruments.

Interest rates

Interest rates have a particularly significant effect on the equity market, more so at the extremes of interest rate cycles and when

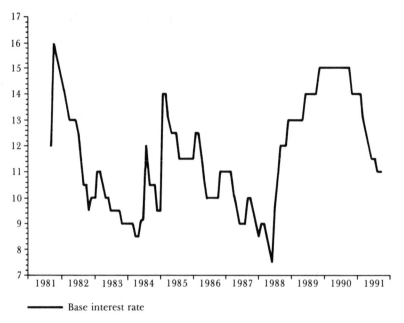

trends are perceived to change (Figure 7.7). Many of the other economic statistics that we have been considering translate their effects directly into short-term interest rates and gilt yields. These pressures then in turn cause larger movements in bank base rates.

Because of the nature of the international financial markets with the ability for rapid movement of money from one currency to another, investors monitor interest rate yields against expected inflation rates and forward exchange rates. All form a vital component in determining whether an Italian investor will get a better return by holding lira in Italy, sterling in London, or dollar deposits.

Gilt yields compared to equities

As the equity market to investors is solely a means of generating dividends and capital growth, it is important to keep a watchful eye on how gilt market returns compare as there is a correlation between the two.

In a risk-free situation, the yield generated by gilts should equal that of equities plus any expected increase in equity dividends over the compared period. As equities do, however, carry a degree of risk they are generally discounted by a 2 per cent risk factor for a more realistic comparison to gilts. We can, therefore, construct an equation:

Gilt yield = equity yield + projected dividend growth − 2% risk factor

The reverse yield gap is defined as the excess of the gilt yield over the equity yield, so gilt and equity returns are equal, after adjusting for risk factors when the reverse yield gap is the same as the expected growth in dividends less the risk factor of 2 per cent.

Thus, if we have an inflation rate of 6 per cent and gross domestic product growth of 3 per cent then dividends can be expected to increase by 9 per cent per year. The reverse yield gap should, therefore, be in the region of 9−2=7 per cent. A higher figure would indicate that equities were overvalued against gilts, while a lower figure would confirm the opposite, so long as GDP growth and inflation rates remain unchanged.

Another way of checking on the relative values of gilts to equities is through the yield-ratio. This is simply the ratio of gilt yields to equity yields. There is no absolute number that such a ratio can be compared to, so in order to determine relative 'cheapness' or 'dearness' of equities to gilts we have to compare our current figure with, say, the average over the last five, or even ten years. If the ratio is above this 'normal' then equities can be considered dear; if it is below the normal then equities may be regarded as cheap.

Figure 7.8 shows an excellent correlation with the equity market crash of October 1987. Prior to that equities were clearly overpriced.

Exchange rates

Traditionally, a strong pound has been good for companies importing goods and raw materials into the UK, while a weak pound gave advantages to exporters. The equities of the companies involved reflected the potential change in profits—i.e. dollar-earning exporters' profits rose sharply as the pound weakened. Since the advent in 1990 of the UK joining the European Monetary System, the potential movement for sterling against its European counterparts has been severely reduced. Companies producing

— Reverse yield gap

Figure 7.8 Reverse yield gap over 10 years
Source: Datastream plc, 1991. Reproduced with permission

goods for the European market must solely rely on selling on the basis of added value and not a cut price as a result of a weakening domestic currency. Against the rest of the world the same old factors still hold, with the proviso that the 'European basket' can be regarded as inherently much more stable—the rest of the world moves up and down against it.

For sterling there has been only a weak correlation between the exchange rate and the volume of international trade. As expected, when sterling strengthens imports rise, but the total effect on the equity market remains minimal. Only when interest rate adjustments have to be made to restore the currency to a more desirable level will the equity market react accordingly.

Economic growth

All the fundamental statistics so far mentioned form part of the jigsaw to help us assess the general health of the economy. Each statistic plays a part of the whole picture and while the individual statistics will be the first to indicate a possible change in the

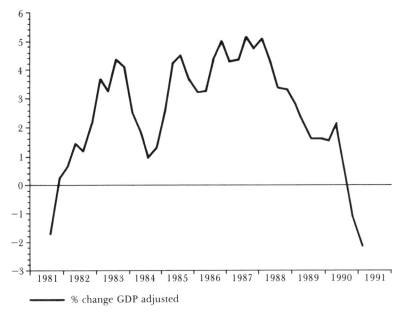

Figure 7.9 GDP over 10 years
Source: Datastream plc, 1991. Reproduced with permission

activity of the economy generally, an individual statistic can also be totally spurious. Aggregated statistics that give an accurate indication of the state of economic activity are of necessity lagging indicators as far as the stock market is concerned. A second problem that arises is the aspect of definition. Just as we briefly glimpsed the almost endless definitions that we can make for 'money in circulation' (much to the delight of the government-controlled statistical office), so with considerations like gross domestic product and consumer expenditure. Nevertheless, these are very important fundamental factors that any longer term investor has to consider, as well as attempt to judge where in the cycle of increasing and decreasing activity we might currently be.

1. GDP

Gross domestic product is the total output of goods and services of the economy (Figure 7.9). In order not to double-count goods of an unfinished or intermediate nature, GDP is defined as the total 'value added' that each manufacturer or producer adds to the goods or services they receive, or have 'input'. Imports are classified as 'input' and, therefore, not counted while exports, as output, are.

GDP can be assessed from the aspects either of income or expenditure GDP. The income measure of GDP is the income generated in the production of the GDP and arises as wages, rentals on land and property, together with profits on invested capital (but excluding interest payments). The income measure of the GDP should theoretically equate to the expenditure on the total output of the GDP, even though other factors will have to be used in its calculation.

GDP can, therefore, become GDP, O, I or E, representing the GDP as calculated on output, income or expenditure. In theory, all will of course be the same, but owing to the difficulties of collating statistics on a national scale, they will always differ in practice. We can, as a result, try to obtain an even better approximation of GDP by averaging the GDP obtained from O, I or E, giving us GDP(A).

Occasionally, and particularly outside the UK, reference is made to GNP or gross national product. This only differs from GDP in that in addition it includes income from investments abroad, less returns on foreign investments, i.e. the net investment income from abroad. Although GDP figures are often subject to revisions, and can be affected to a certain degree by political manipulation, the rate of growth of the economy is, nevertheless, still the most important indicator of economic performance. Comparisons of GDP figures for different countries provide instant ranking of countries by economic activity. Equities will tend to show greater capital growth where GDP is the highest. If GDP figures indicate steady growth, equities will continue to flourish; when the GDP indicates a decrease in the rate of growth (or even decline) bear markets are seen.

As a short-term trading indicator, GDP is not used. It is, however, the major confirmer that a particular economic cycle is under way, speeding up or slowing down. As such, it is one of the most important statistics that one should watch.

2. Consumers' expenditure

Often easier to relate to than the GDP is the amount of money that an individual has to spend (Figure 7.10). Personal income, which

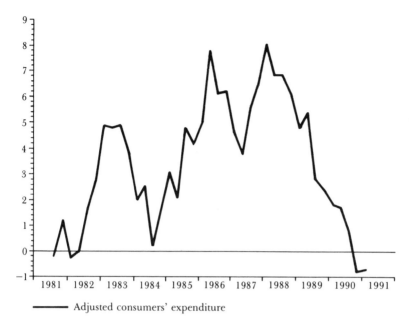

Figure 7.10 Consumers' expenditure over 10 years
Source: Datastream plc, 1991. Reproduced with permission

becomes personal disposable income (PDI) after tax deductions, accounts for the largest part of the economy and is also a better guide to changes in living standards than the GDP. By definition, that part of personal disposable income that is not saved becomes consumers' expenditure, and consumers' expenditure on goods and services account for about 65 per cent of the GDP (as measured directly by expenditure). Figures showing consumers' expenditure, which to a large degree will be mirrored in retail sales, give a direct view of the state of the economy and whether demand for goods and services is increasing or decreasing. Published figures are seasonally adjusted in order to smooth out the large increase in purchases made during the fourth quarter, ahead of Christmas. As a fundamental indicator of the equity market, consumers' expenditure gives a quicker signal than the more encompassing GNP; it can also be broken down by sector to show which sections of the economy are performing best.

3. Stockbuilding

Figures published for stockbuilding are often volatile and can be interpreted in different ways in different parts of the economic cycle, i.e. large stocks of finished goods can mean either a collapse of sales or increased production anticipating increasing demand. Interpretation is also confused because of the difficulties of stock valuation and taxation allowances.

Stockbuilding is seen in three main areas, each accounting for about a third of the total—raw materials and fuel, work-in-progress and finished goods. As demand picks up, stocks of finished goods will be the first to decline, thus generating an increase in work-in-progress. High interest rates, however, make it expensive for companies to carry excessive stock, and lower stocks can also reflect an organization's increased efficiency in securing raw materials or components at a much more rapid rate. Published stockbuilding figures must, therefore, be interpreted alongside other economic statistics, but as such they give a very good indication of what may be happening at the factory floor level, and so give a strong signal as to how equity markets may be likely to develop.

A fundamental view of fundamental factors

Over the last decade much more weight is being placed on fundamental economic indicators by the financial markets, politicians and the media. An increasingly large section of the general public is becoming aware of how certain economic statistics may affect them directly—especially an increasing cycle of unemployment, decreasing interest rates, mortgage rates and changing house prices. Consequently, these monthly and quarterly statistical snapshots that government economic departments publish become, for an instant, an important 'story' that politicians of all persuasions can use to confirm the soundness of their own views! This overdramatization of individual statistics by the press and politicians goes hand in hand with the very large market moves often seen the instant figures are published. For most market 'locals', and many active traders, published figures become a focal point for a bit of very short-term, highly speculative activity, activity that in some instances may only endure for a few seconds.

Table 7.1 Fundamental influence summary

Economic factor	Effect on stock market
Average earnings	Rise in average earnings at start of economic cycle is positive to equities, later negative
Balance of payments	Positive balance is positive for equities
Consumers' expenditure	Both rise together but will be stock specific
Exchange rate	A weakening currency may signal higher interest rates and so be bad for equities
GDP	Minimal, tends to lag behind stock market
Interest rates	Decreasing rates are positive for equities
Manufacturing production	Increase will be positive for equities
PSBR	Small or negative PSBR is positive for equities
Retail prices	Higher retail prices may depress equities in short term, longer term not so important
Stockbuilding levels	Various, specific to business and position in economic cycle. Can give very good market signals
Unemployment	Lagging indicator for equity market

Economic figures under these circumstances have become the object of a new speculative game not dissimilar to betting on the outcome of a horse race.

The sweet irony of all this activity is that while the result of a horse race is seldom altered by a stewards' enquiry, economic statistics are subject to constant revision. Initial statistics are often the 'best-estimate' at the time when they 'have' to be announced, and consequently can be wildly inaccurate. Subsequent revisions, of which there can be many, improve the quality of the information provided, and a better and better insight of how an economy is working is obtained over a period of time. Although revisions of economic statistics can be very large, and can even negate the instant interpretation of the original numbers, they do not attract anything like the speculative response of the initial publications. For the longer term investor, statistical revisions are as important as any other numbers in giving a series of numerical snapshots with which to interpret the progress of the economic cycle.

With the present, almost global vogue for privatization and economic deregulation, it is becoming more difficult for accurate statistical analysis to be carried out. Just as the profitability of a company cannot be judged only on the tax that it pays (some argue that tax paid is a measure of inefficiency), so every economic statistic has to be seen in the light of its own information limits. Statistical information from thousands of diverse small companies can be virtually impossible to collate; large organizations moving from the public to the private sector can cause distortions in, for instance, the PSBR; innovations in the banking sector, like the introduction of the credit card, can cause massive changes in money supply. At the same time we are moving to a more open society where more and more 'information' is available to everyone. For the fundamental investor, the constant problem is that more and more does not necessarily mean better and better, the danger is that more information may give rise to more confusion.

CHAPTER 8

Trading

All market activity can be regarded as 'trading'. We shall now, however, consider index trading strategies as opposed to hedging strategies, which will be dealt with in the next chapter. As more complex strategies are considered it becomes clear that there is no simple division line between trading and hedging—the two techniques overlap and merge, aside from any switching of emphasis such as when a short-term investment becomes a long-term hedge (often for rather poor reasons), or a long-term hedge is suddenly turned into an instant speculative profit.

Using futures and options contracts to create trading returns is the easiest of all the strategies to understand but by far the most difficult in which to gain proficiency. The simple opening of a position, in order to make a profit from one's market view, very quickly forces one to consider the well-established disciplines associated with successful speculation. For many fund managers the very term 'speculation' is anathema. They are charged with the prudent care of public funds, and in many cases can be compared to curators of a national monument, they need a long-term view. The fund that they have to manage, such as a pension fund, was probably in existence long before they were made responsible for it. After spending some time caring for it, and possibly adapting it a little to meet current circumstances, they hand it on for a new manager to nurture. The pension fund will probably be in thriving existence long after many generations of fund managers have ceased to require a pension themselves. Speculation, and indeed any form of risk, has no place in such long-term financial commitments.

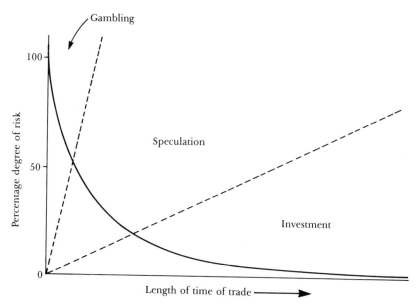

Figure 8.1 Risk-time profile (gambling, speculating and investing)

Yes and no. For many investors the arguments come down to problems of definition. If we accept that *all* investments carry some degree of risk, it is only a short step to declare that all investment is speculation. Clearly an uncomfortable conclusion. The arguments can, however, be resolved if we consider the degree of risk accepted over a particular time period (Figure 8.1).

At the top of the graph, where the degree of risk is 100 per cent over a very short time frame, comes gambling. At the other end of the range where risk is almost zero (governments have at times failed to honour their borrowings), we can put long-term investment in gilts, Treasury Bills, etc. Other investments find their place somewhere in between, although a so-called safe investment vehicle such as a gilt can become a highly speculative instrument when used via a futures or options position over a short-term trading view. Different investors will in any case have different time frame objectives. At the other end of the time scale to the pension fund manager is the 'local' in the trading pit who will have a short-term view of the market, about 30 seconds, and a long-term view rarely greater than three or four hours. The diversity of time frame requirements from different investors will all contribute to the overall activity and liquidity of the market, and each may exert a significant effect on market movement. For these reasons, all investors need to have an understanding of the disciplines that short-term traders will be attempting to adhere to. More significantly, long-term investments benefit from the same management disciplines that are used by the more successful speculators; only the time frame is different.

The disciplines of trading

If we assume that we have access to all the best available fundamental analyses together with all the appropriate technical timing indicators, we still cannot be totally certain of how the market will move tomorrow, and how tomorrow will affect the rest of the decade. Consequently, while paying regard to technical and fundamental considerations, it is actually 'technique' that plays a major part in the success of any short-term investment. Good trading technique is neither magic nor esoteric science. It is based on the simple observation that in order to make money out of trading, our profits must consistently be larger than our losses. In order to achieve this, all we have to do is to make sure that our losses stay small by liquidating 'wrong' positions, and nurture our profits so that they are taken either at predetermined levels on a rise or at protective levels on setbacks. All trading systems are designed to this simple discipline using differing techniques and mathematical models that supposedly give the 'best' signals for a particular commodity or stock index. Whenever a market develops a strong trend, such as we see in almost all equity markets once or twice a year, all trading systems, as well as our disciplined speculator, should make a very healthy return on investment. At other times, when the market is keeping within a range and giving many false signals, small profits will probably be more than offset by many small losses. At times like these the disciplined speculator trading on the 'feel' of the market often has better results than many purely mechanical systems.

While the theory behind the technique of speculation is so simple, 'run your profits and cut your losses', the plans for achieving this are legion. Some are better for one commodity than another, for one stock index rather than another, and will differ from one individual to another. Some will work for a time and then appear to lose their ability to give good buy or sell signals. For the individual, however, there are only two reasons why 85 per cent of short-term traders consistently lose money.

1. Lack of trading plan   We can toss a coin to decide whether to buy or sell. What we do after that must be decided in advance— where do we decide that we are wrong and cut our losses, and where do we either take our profits or make new decisions about protecting increasing profits?

2. Lack of discipline to stick to the trading plan   To help the speculative trader develop a trading plan there are a number of questions that should be considered. The list that follows is not to be regarded as absolute, and not in any order of importance. Speculation is a totally personal activity. The persistent speculator will in time learn which points are the more important for his own benefit. Different psychological approaches may be required when dealing with institutional funds—where the risk-reward may be between getting to keep one's job or securing a large bonus and, for one's own investments, where on the one hand we may lose money so that it hurts, or win so much that we improve our way of life. In all cases the battle is between varying degrees of fear and greed.

Principles to consider before opening short-term trades

1. What is the major trend in the market, and what is the short-term trend? Is the envisaged investment period compatible with the perceived trend for that period? Attempting to spot the tops and bottoms in the market is statistically disadvantageous.
2. What money management techniques are being employed, in other words, what proportion of available capital is being committed to a single trade? If all available capital is placed on an investment where the outcome is total loss or a double, sooner or later ruin is inevitable. If only 10 per cent of available speculative capital is placed in each investment, the chances of finding a strong favourable trend are greatly increased.
3. What is the profit objective of the trade? If the maximum objective is similar to the possible loss then it is wrong to trade.
4. At what level of loss can the original investment decision be

regarded as wrong and, therefore, closed with a predetermined and hence controlled loss?

5. Should stop-loss orders be placed as levels decided in 4? Stop-loss orders should not be removed once placed. The reason for placing a stop is to limit a loss because an investment position has been opened wrongly. While all users of stops will have experiences of seeing their stops triggered, only to see the market reverse direction subsequently, far more memorable losses can be created by having no stops at all. The many more occasions when stops do in fact close out wrong investments and preserve much of the trader's capital, tend to be forgotten.

6. Avoiding running a profit into a loss. Every speculative position is at its most vulnerable until it has reached its minimum profit objective. Once at this point, the profit must either be realized or protected through the use of stop-loss orders, in this case being used as 'stop-profit' orders. Such stop-profit orders can be ratcheted up should our bullish position start to advance to even higher levels.

7. Having clear reasons why we open or close positions. This can be especially difficult to decide on very profitable positions. The prospect of a large return can be very tempting but why get out if the market is still trending strongly in the same direction.

8. Avoiding the natural bias to always want to be long. Profits are often generated at a faster rate for bear positions in bear markets than for bull positions in bull markets.

9. There is no benefit to be gained by being in the market the whole time. When the investor has no opinion on the direction of the market one should wait until a pattern or trend develops.

10. Averaging a loss can be dangerous. For a large institution with a long-time horizon, averaging down, i.e. buying more as the market declines, is a legitimate strategy. For a smaller investor or fund, this can be another path to ruin.

11. Trading on one's own opinions after considering the input from all possible sources. Following the leads of others numbs one's senses and prevents one from developing one's own market feel. A committee has never been a successful vehicle for generating a constant stream of profitable trading decisions.

Time frames

We have considered some of the principles that a short-term trader might employ to monitor trading activity. Most of the same principles will apply to long-term investments as well as very short-term ones, but there will be differences. For any investor to be in control of events, an understanding is required of the objectives that drive investors with different time frame horizons. We saw from Figure 8.1 that the differences between gambling, speculation and investment were only those of degree of risk over a period of time. In Chapter 1 we saw how early problems with the definition of the word 'gambling' actually held up the development of stock index trading. Speculation is now regarded as any investment involving a high degree of risk but with the opportunity of making considerable profits. Pure 'investment' takes the longer term view and does not seek risk. And yet, as we shall now consider, short-term, medium-term and long-term traders may all be trading at the same time, taking similar *or* opposite market views, and benefiting from being aware of who is probably doing what and why.

Pit trading, the short-term view

Although a few investors buying and selling stock index futures or options contracts will be doing so for short-term speculative gain, the majority will have longer time horizons for their strategies. Not so the many traders in the pit. These pit traders, either locals or company employees with dealing limits, will be looking to make trading profits out of very short-time horizons. In the case of 'scalpers', these horizons may average open positions of no more than a few minutes.

Several other diametrically opposed outlooks exist between the traders in the pit and investors primarily concerned with managing equity portfolios. 'Investors' will be concerned about basis risk. They will wish to buy index futures at or below fair-value and sell the same at or above fair-value. Pit traders care little for such theoretical considerations. Many short-term traders, in fact, prefer to buy expensive futures with the thought that increasing premium increases interest, which in turn will guarantee a ready supply of longer term investors seeking to pick up cheaper stock on setbacks.

These investors to a large extent protect the locals by giving them the chance of liquidating their long positions in seconds whenever the more aggressive buying pressure eases back.

Many pit traders take pride in the attitude that they have no real opinion on the direction in which the market might be moving. They are purely reacting to the market forces that they see at work during their time scale. By the same token a major investor will be able to give fundamental and technical reasons as to why the market will go to new highs over the next six months; however, he will have little of value to say if asked to give his opinion on the likely movement of the market over the next 90 seconds. And yet many locals make a very good living out of the market with no more than a 90-second view at any time. It seems very curious that both are trading the same market, both can make good returns and yet each have not a clue as to what the other is doing or thinking.

This short-time horizon is the key to pit trading psychology. If a trader can see the market rising two index points on the FT-SE 100 Index future and he buys 10 futures contracts at 2457, a sale made at 2459 will net a profit of £500 in the space of not many seconds. One only needs to spot an opportunity like this once or twice a day to secure a very reasonable standard of living.

A far less risky pastime that pit traders indulge in is 'scalping'. The market will always have a bid and an offer. If there is reasonable activity without much market movement, traders can spend many happy hours buying at the bid and selling at the offer. The activity is so attractive that even among pit traders there is some competition to be able to do this, but so long as there is a spread between the bid and the offer the odds will always favour the scalper.

While many pit traders will have no opinion on the market in its macro-view, they often have pretty good ideas as to where the immediate market forces in the pit will be pushing them. From experience they will know who are the dealers that handle major institutional business, and often have some idea as to which way it may be depending on the market at the time, or the particular way that the telephone clerk swallows hard as he makes a note of the new order. Pit traders will also develop their opinions on who in the pit may be holding large buy or sell orders close to current market levels. Just as a bridge player will be counting the cards played in order to assess where the last trumps are held, some traders will be working out in their minds just who is likely to want to cover a particular position before the end of the day.

The longer time horizon

For the fund manager these considerations may appear far removed from his own activity. Actually this is not quite so. The difference is only that of time horizon. A fund manager needs to be aware, in exactly the same way as the pit local, of who is doing what in his time frame and scale. This helps one to assess what the other major players may be doing in the market. Whether index funds are buying because the future is cheap, is arbitrage activity in one direction or another, and what may therefore happen at contract expiry, from which fund managers are likely to benefit.

One major difference does exist. The very short time horizon under which pit traders operate ensures that we can see who is successful and get some ideas of the techniques that those traders are using. Unsuccessful pit traders last a very short length of time. The wily 'older' traders who have lasted for many years are the ones that we can learn from the most. Regrettably, by the same argument, successful fund managers take years to develop and are often only recognized after half a lifetime!

Locals in the trading pit are no different to any trader who is seeking to generate a more substantial profit by capturing a large part of a favourable trend. Again only the time frame will be different in each case. Once the market has established a direction, one only needs to go with it to make a profit. The herd instinct is a very powerful force in this respect, and any experienced trader will know not to fight the trend. Difficulties arise when we try to spot a trend—who is likely to be a trendsetter with so many keen followers?

On a macro-scale a trend is easy to see. Any chart of any equity market will usually show two or three significant trends in any one year. A pit trader will also be aware of overall movement, but will initially seek a trend that lasts to lunchtime. These mini-trends will also have their support and resistance areas of which traders will be wary. Different techniques can be used for very short-term views; some traders will be watching to see what volume trades at particular levels and for how long. Few, however, will be market leaders. The 5, 20 or even 100 lots that the larger locals may trade will only move the market a limited amount. Even all the locals together going in one direction create an unbalanced move that is safe only to those in last and out first. Important trends actually start by the actions of the larger investors. A good local or pit trader may be astute enough to anticipate major institutional buying or selling, but it is the larger orders placed in the pit that mop up all the offers and cause prices to rise, attracting more buyers on the grounds that prices are starting to rise. Further momentum is created by positions being carried forward.

Major trends will then develop only if a majority of large market players, for often differing reasons, do the same thing. The herd instinct again, but now on a gigantic scale. We still have not, however, identified the actual trigger that started the trend. Sometimes it is easy to see—an unexpected interest rate cut or a major takeover bid can galvanize the market into action, not just for a few minutes but can actually ratchet the market to new higher levels over a period of days or weeks. At other times, these same actions have no more effect than to create the pit traders' great joy—the 30-second strong trend followed by the 2-minute reversal. What is a trend trigger on one occasion may be nothing of the kind on another. When the market wants bad news in order to confirm a downward path, it will often ignore news that in a bull market would have caused the remaining bears to become desperate coverers of their short positions. A major trend is created by a host of bits of information that cause a number of significant investors to act in similar fashion, causing this fashion to develop into the right thing for all to do.

Pit traders and fund managers may in many respects be worlds apart but the aims of all are similar—to use the market in a beneficial manner. It can only be of help in pursuing one's own goals if one understands the psychology of the other, all the players in the market depending on each other for the system to work.

Having covered some of the aspects of simple position taking, we can now look at all the other facets of employing a trading view in various strategies.

Using gearing to enhance returns

If a fund manager believes strongly that the market is due to rise, he can, through using futures, cause his fund to increase in value at a greater rate than the simple market rise.

Example

Let us assume that the fund has £9 000 000 invested in a broad range of equities, and £1 000 000 on deposit earning interest of 12 per cent per year. The market rises 10 per cent over a three-month period.

Case 1   The fund manager does nothing. At the end of the three-month period his fund will be worth:

$$£9\ 000\ 000 + (£9\ 000\ 000 \times 10\%) = £\ 9\ 900\ 000$$

$$£1\ 000\ 000 + \left(\frac{£1\ 000\ 000 \times 12\%}{4}\right) = £\ 1\ 030\ 000$$

$$\text{Total} = £10\ 930\ 000$$

A gain of 9.3 per cent when the market has risen 10 per cent.

Case 2   The fund manager removes the cash on deposit and uses all of this money as margin for futures contracts. Assuming margin required is £2 000 per contract, he can, therefore, buy:

$$\frac{£1\ 000\ 000}{£2\ 000} = 500 \text{ futures contracts}$$

The FT-SE Index then rises 10 per cent, from 2800 to 3080. The fund will now be worth:

$$£9\ 000\ 000 + (£9\ 000\ 000 \times 10\%) = £\ 9\ 900\ 000$$

$$500 \times (3080 - 2800) \times £25 \qquad = £\ 3\ 500\ 000$$

$$\text{Total} = £13\ 400\ 000$$

The £25 is of course the contract size, i.e. the value per index point, and the gain of 34 per cent that the fund demonstrates is due to the increased gearing. The 500 futures contracts provided an equity equivalent investment value of:

$$500 \times 2800 \times \text{£}25 = \text{£}35\,000\,000$$

much larger than the original fund.

Case 3 The fund manager decides on limited gearing and only purchases 100 futures contracts requiring a margin of: $100 \times \text{£}2000 = \text{£}200000$. In this instance, after a market rise of 10 per cent the fund value will be:

$$\text{£}9\,000\,000 + (\text{£}9\,000\,000 \times 10\%) = \text{£}\ 9\,900\,000$$

$$\text{£}800\,000 + \left(\frac{\text{£}800\,000 \times 12\%}{4}\right) = \text{£}\quad 824\,000$$

$$100 \times (3080 - 2800) \times \text{£}25 \quad = \text{£}\quad 700\,000$$

$$\text{Total} = \text{£}11\,424\,000$$

This situation gives a gain of 14.24 per cent, a lower gain than in Case 2 because our futures equity equivalent is only $100 \times 2800 \times \text{£}25 = \text{£}7\,000\,000$. In both these two latter cases the fund has been geared up to give a greater return than would otherwise have been achieved, even if all the fund was invested in equities. Gearing is, however, a two-edged sword—a badly judged futures investment left unchecked would give geared losses of identical magnitude for similar market moves in the other direction.

Index fund enhancement

In Chapter 3 we looked at fair-value and its use in determining arbitrage opportunities. There are, of course, several other strategies that depend on fair-value considerations.

Any fund that is index-related, or contains an identifiable index element, can have its value enhanced by the strategic use of stock index contracts. An index fund manager with money to invest in the index should always look at how the futures contract is trading. Should the futures contract be at a discount to its fair-value then, by buying the futures contract instead of the equities that make up the index, we are actually buying the same equities at a discount. When the futures contract expires at parity with the index, or earlier if there is an opportunity to sell the futures contract at its fair-value or even above its fair-value, then the equities that were originally desired should be purchased. Whatever has happened to the market during the interim, the net result is a gain over where we would have been if we had just purchased the equities originally. It must be remembered in transactions of this nature that futures contracts are opened on the basis of a margin deposit. The difference between the underlying value of a futures contract and its margin must of course be invested in short-term credit instruments, the interest so earned will offset the lack of dividend income and the erosion of the fair futures premium.

Example

A fund manager has to invest £12 000 000 into an index tracking fund which correlates with the FT-SE 100 Index. The futures contract is trading at 2860, 35 points below its fair-value with still two months before expiry of the futures contract.

The fund manager buys:

$$\frac{£12\ 000\ 000}{2860 \times £25} = 168\ \text{futures contracts}$$

The fund gains in that an equity equivalent investment has been made at a 35 index point discount, a value of $35 \times 168 \times £25 = £147\ 000$.

On expiry of the futures contract, which will be at fair-value or earlier if possible, equities are purchased in the normal way to realize the 'bonus'. Alternatively, if the next future is trading below its fair-value, more outperformance can be added by rolling from the near to the next contract.

The gain so realized by this strategy must be considered against the ease with which equities may be purchased at the time of the transaction or at a later date, and also how close the FT-SE 100 index tracks the fund under management. Nevertheless, the gain is a real one and of value to most index tracking funds as unbalanced elements in funds can be restored by the separate investments in a limited number of suitable equities.

By the same reasoning, if we need to generate cash by liquidating an equity portfolio, and the future is trading substantially above fair-value, we may actually be better off borrowing the cash that we may need and selling futures contracts to the appropriate underlying value. Once the futures contract falls back to or below its fair-value the entire position is unwound and again we have made a positive contribution to our overall performance.

The beauty of these strategies is that they are only employed when enhanced performance is guaranteed. If nothing is to be gained by using the futures contract we simply limit our activity to the equity market.

Investment of a dividend stream

Often a fund, after years of careful management, will have what is perceived to be an 'ideal' balance of equities. The fund, however, generates a constant stream of dividends that need to be invested back into the fund. It is impractical, however, to spread the dividends across the entire fund by purchasing small quantities of shares in possibly several hundred different companies. To purchase sensible numbers of shares in just a few companies will upset the balance of the portfoloio. By far the most sensible route is to purchase stock index futures contracts to the underlying value of the sum to be invested and place the differential between the underlying value and the margin requirement on short-term deposit. We thus have exposure to the entire FT-SE 100 Share Index. Once our investment via the futures contract is large enough to sensibly invest in the range of equities required by the fund, the futures position is liquidated and equities purchased.

If we have been fortunate to purchase the index futures contracts at a discount to fair-value, then our 'synthetic' fund will have outperformed the index element of the equity fund (or the entire fund if it is an index fund). This, however, is a bonus. The reason for the strategy is to increase market exposure in a balanced way. For this facility a fund manager should be prepared to pay a certain level of premium over fair-value. A general rule here is that as dealing costs on equities are 1.4 per cent of the value and futures only 0.12 per cent (see Chapter 3) if we are using futures for convenience over equities we could pay up to 1.4 per cent − 0.12 per cent = 1.28 per cent over fair-value, or 32 points above fair-value at an index level of 2500.

Synthetic index funds A further extension to the ideas considered in the last section gives us a totally equity-free index fund, or synthetic index fund—total participation in the equity market without buying or selling stocks. We buy stock index futures and invest the differential between the underlying equity equivalent value and the margin requirement in short-term credit instruments such as certificates of deposit. So long as we invest at fair-value on the futures market, roll our quarterly contracts at fair-value, and secure a competitive rate of interest on our deposits, we shall match the performance of the index as if we had been invested in all the equities of the index in their correct weightings so as to duplicate the index.

What can go wrong? In the ideal circumstances of the future trading at fair-value, nothing. Our only risk is basis risk, i.e. the future trading expensively whenever we wish to purchase futures contracts or roll positions, and trading below fair-value just when we need to sell positions. If our synthetic index fund, however, is expected to exist for a period of years rather than months, then basis risk is evened out. There should be as many times that we invest expensively as cheaply, and roll our quarterly contracts with gain as with loss. So here we have a passive fund that requires a minimum of monitoring and will perform in line with the index without any stocks.

There is every reason why a passive fund of this nature may actually outperform the index. Although 'passive', there is still an element of choice as to whether to purchase stock index futures at one time or another. If possible, investments should be made at times when the future is trading cheap. Roll over periods can be used to attempt to add value, i.e. anomalously low-cost spread trades can be picked up when they occur, anomalously high levels do not have to be chased. If the spread differential is increasing, it may be wise to roll the entire position as soon as possible. If it is decreasing, it will be advantageous to hold back and roll the position in small lots hoping to gain more benefit as the forward contract reduces in premium.

As we are dealing with quarterly futures contracts, our non-margin cash should also be invested in three-month certificates of deposit and 'rolled' for a new three-month period in line with the stock index contract. There will be small variations between the rate of interest that banks will offer so here again is an opportunity to add value. A policy decision to invest not in bank CDs but in 'riskier' deposit takers like building societies or local authorities can add further value to our index fund.

Cost considerations of synthetic funds

A major advantage that synthetic funds will have over equity-based funds is that of management cost.

An equity-based 'index' fund will have far higher dealing charges (commissions and dealing spreads) than a futures contract based fund. While an equity or futures fund may be actually managed by an individual of similar calibre, the equity fund will suffer higher infrastructure costs of research staff and accounting, the passive synthetic fund needing no equity research or procedures for handling dividends. Where the synthetic fund really does score is when we look to expand our expertise into other markets. With little extra expense our synthetic fund manager can purchase Nikkei-Dow futures and make three-month yen deposits, thereby creating instant exposure to the Japanese index.

Similarly, we can obtain market exposure to the American market, French market, German market or any other market that has a stock index futures contract that is representative of its domestic equity market. This futures market investment route is far cheaper than employing stock-picking experts for each overseas investment location, buying the equities, monitoring the results, and watching the average fund manager underperforming against the index. Using synthetic equity funds we are virtually certain to match the index, and if we are modestly fortunate we can even outperform it, without having to know anything at all about the stocks that make up the overseas equity markets.

Partial synthetic funds

Earlier in this chapter we looked at how a dividend stream might be invested in the 'total' market via the stock index futures contract. In this instance we actually had an equity fund with a synthetic element. It is not difficult to see that this synthetic element can grow and grow, particularly if it is outperforming the main fund and both fund managers and trustees are becoming more confident that the futures contract can be used in a non-speculative manner. It has been particularly difficult in the UK to establish totally synthetic funds in the past, whereas a synthetic element has been easier to justify on the grounds that one is not risking the entire pension fund on the futures market—only the bit that is growing out of new dividends.

Now that the laws of taxation of derivative instruments have been brought in line (in 1990) with general practice in other developed parts of the world, and derivative instruments are seen to be able to add value or facilitate more complex strategies at reasonable cost, considerable growth in partial and total synthetic funds is being seen.

Synthetic index funds can also be used to provide the mainstay of an investment, i.e. performance generally in line with the index, but allowing investment managers (as opposed to just 'fund' managers) to add value to the overall fund by increasing exposure to those equities that are expected to perform better than the index. This seems an eminently sensible route for investment to take. Take out the day-to-day worries of trying to perform as well as the index by creating a synthetic index fund; then add value by over-exposing to special situations or opportunities that are expected to perform better than the norm. For our derivative instrument fund to be 'complete' it only needs, where possible, for outperformance to be sought via the options and warrants market, and the reduced costs of dealing in these instruments can be partially translated into increased gearing.

Asset allocation using futures

Much research has been done by investment analysts on the ideal ways of allocating a portfolio's total assets between equities, gilts or bonds and short-term credit instruments. Much less has been written on the most efficient ways of switching asset allocations as the cycles of economic change create new investment climates. Usually, an investment manager will restructure his portfolio by buying and selling individual equities, liquidating equity positions in favour of gilts and cash (short-term deposits) or reducing short-term deposits in favour of increased equity exposure. However, by using stock index futures contracts and interest rate futures contracts it is possible to change the portfolio's asset allocation without the need to purchase or sell large numbers of equities.

Futures contracts are particularly efficient at portfolio restructuring for the following reasons:

1. Stock index and interest rate futures markets are now liquid enough to accept sizeable trades quickly.
2. Costs of trading futures, as seen earlier, are much less than those of trading individual stocks and gilts or bonds.
3. The futures contracts employed are broadly representative of the areas between which assets are to be transferred. Gilt and bond futures will very closely replicate the movements of the underlying cash instruments. Although pension fund managers in the UK tend to use the All Share Index as a yardstick for performance, the FT-SE 100 Index has a 98 per cent correlation with the All Share. This may not be acceptable to funds on a time frame of over six months, but the speed of transaction allows almost instant change in asset allocation, which can then be fine-tuned at a more leisurely rate once it is decided which specific equities are to be bought or sold.
4. In large organizations where several individuals are responsible for different investment vehicles, the senior fund manager can manage the asset mix of a portfolio without disrupting the day-to-day activities of investment managers.

Example using futures to change asset allocation mix

A pension fund of £1 billion has 60 per cent invested in equities, 25 per cent in gilts and 15 per cent on short-term deposit. A decision is taken to alter the asset mix to 50 per cent equities, 30 per cent gilts and 20 per cent on deposit. Therefore, to restructure the portfolio, the pension fund manager must reduce his exposure to equities by £100 million and increase investment in gilt stock by £50 million. The usual way of doing this would be to select a range of equities to sell and with the funds so generated to purchase gilts, leaving £50 million extra as cash on deposit.

By using gilt and stock index futures contracts we can also implement this change. The portfolio's exposure to the stock market is changed by selling the correct quantity of stock index futures contracts to offset the risk of a £100 million equity position. With the index at 2650 and the value of the futures contract being worth £25 per point, the number of futures contracts required to be sold is:

$$\frac{100\,000\,000}{2650 \times 25} = 1509 \text{ to the nearest contract}$$

The number of long gilt futures contracts is similarly calculated although it has to be adjusted by a price factor that converts a gilt futures price into an equivalent price for the gilt actually delivered. It represents the price per £1 nominal of the gilt at which it yields 8 per cent on the first day of the delivery month. For the purposes of the example we shall assume a price factor of 1. The number of long gilt futures required is therefore:

$$\frac{£50\,000\,000}{£50\,000} \times 1 = 1000 \text{ contracts}$$

The desired asset allocation has been achieved 'synthetically' and relatively quickly. The fund manager can now decide whether to reverse his futures positions as he makes measured changes to his equity and gilt positions, retaining his futures positions on the grounds that the equity position is well balanced and too cumbersome to reduce in a sensible manner, particularly should there be a later change in strategy that requires increased investment in equities.

As well as the major asset allocation changes we have just looked at, futures can also be used on a more regular, small-scale basis in order to make, say, quarterly adjustments to a portfolio. A constant problem for the fund manager is to maintain a predetermined asset mix under the handicap of an unending waterfall of cash in the form of dividends, interest and new investment, all conspiring to upset the balance by boosting cash deposits. Using futures contracts, the required balance of the fund can be maintained as a matter of course by making small adjustments, if need be, on a monthly or even weekly basis.

Global asset allocation

Earlier in this chapter we saw how easily we could create 'synthetic' index funds in any stock market that has a stock index futures contract. We can also use these same futures contracts to alter the investment balance of international or continental funds.

Example

A fund manager with a £500 million portfolio plans to keep 60 per cent invested in the USA and 40 per cent in the Japanese market. The fund is valued in sterling. After a period of considerable Japanese growth at a greater rate than the American market the manager now has a fund worth £620 million but split 55/45, i.e. the US part is worth £341 million, the Japanese element £279 million. To restore the portfolio to its desired balance he must sell £31 million of Japanese equities and purchase this amount of American ones. With the Nikkei-Dow stock index future at 31 050, the contract valued at ¥500 per point, and the sterling yen exchange rate at 271.80, we should need to sell the following number of Japanese stock index futures contracts:

$$\text{each contract value} = \frac{31\,050 \times 500}{271.80} = £57\,119.205$$

$$\frac{31\,000\,000}{57\,119.205} = 543 \text{ to the nearest contract}$$

A similar calculation to purchase £31 million of S & P 500 futures is made with the S & P 500 at 345.70, worth $500 per point and the exchange rate at £1 = $1.8500:

$$\text{each contract is worth:} \frac{345.70 \times 500}{1.8500} = £93\,432.43$$

$$\frac{31\,000\,000}{93432.43} = 332 \text{ to the nearest contract}$$

A change of asset allocation of this nature, allowing for time zone differentials, will still only take a maximum of 24 hours and more normally half a working day. The expense and difficulty of dealing in the equities of overseas markets is obviated.

For the active European fund with over a dozen different stock markets to follow, the simplicity that stock index contracts provide for changing asset allocations between countries is even more apparent.

Synthetic warrant funds

Similarly to synthetic futures funds that seek to track or even sometimes outperform a portfolio of physical equities, fund managers can also use warrants to maximize performance by the creation of a synthetic warrant fund. A fund of this nature will have certain advantages over a synthetic futures fund in that gearing advantages can be even more attractive, while the time frame that warrants employ will mean that the constant rolling of quarterly futures contracts is obviated. Against this have to be set the higher initial warrant costs.

A synthetic warrant fund is created by simply selling the portfolio of stocks in the original index fund and buying the correct amount of index warrants to maintain the required degree of exposure. The balance of the money is put on deposit. This strategy will give a fixed return on the cash on deposit and the opportunity of a superior performance from the warrants over the index, if there are large index level movements during the life of the warrants. One of two techniques can then be employed to monitor the investment position—a static or dynamic approach.

Static approach   After the warrants have been purchased and cash put on deposit, nothing more needs to be done until the end of the designated period (possibly the moment of warrant maturity). Then the warrants, if profitable, are sold, the cash removed from deposit, and the total sum reinvested so that the original portfolio of equities is restored. The object of the exercise is, of course, that we now hold a larger portfolio than we would have done if we had not done anything at all to the original portfolio.

Dynamic approach   Dynamic investment, as the name suggests, means that the warrant position is actively managed to maximize on all possibilities. Unlike the static approach, if the index had shown a large fall, the warrant might temporarily be almost valueless, but the overall position would still be far better than if entirely invested in equities. At this point the fund manager might decide to buy another call warrant, so that when the market recovers, the extra leverage produces a far higher return than might otherwise have been expected.

Alternatively, we could strive to use warrants in order to maintain a delta neutral position. As the share price falls, warrants are purchased so that a delta neutral position is restored (after particular, predetermined percentage falls). As the level of the index rises, warrants are then sold in order, again, to achieve delta neutrality.

One problem that can arise here is that to allow for dealing costs of commissions and spreads, a movement of at least 5 per cent must be seen in the index level. Furthermore, because cash may be needed for more warrant purchases, there may be penalties to pay when cash that would otherwise have been placed on long-term deposit, only carries overnight rates of interest.

These handicaps accepted, it is sometimes a mystery why any fund manager struggles along with equities when a warrant strategy such as this or even a similar, actively managed synthetic futures fund, could significantly outperform a pure equity fund. Usually the reasons are twofold. Senior fund management, by its very nature and calling, must be conservative in its approach, with new ideas having to be proved over time. This, however, is severely handicapped by the second reason—that of a general ignorance (now being thankfully eroded) of the real nature and strategic possibilities of derivative products.

Cash-baskets and index participations

Further instruments that sometimes offer advantages to index tracking funds are 'cash-baskets' and 'index participations'.

Cash-baskets are best regarded as a portfolio of equities that represent either a sector or a particular index. The actual equities do not have to be purchased to create the cash-basket, but buyers and sellers must be aware of exactly what constitutes the basket, i.e. the companies included and exactly how many shares in each company are required. The cash-basket can be a unique basket of shares, but more usually it will be a basket of equities that corresponds to a particular known index. It is, therefore, a standard parcel of shares that can be traded, the changing value of the basket mirroring the subsequent changes in the values of the constituent equities.

This predetermined basket of equities can now be traded, the difference with the futures contract being that instead of trading on a margin, the buyer has to pay the total value of the basket of equities. The buyer will also receive such dividends as the portfolio of equities generates while the portfolio is in the buyer's possession. On the other hand, the seller of the basket receives the cash but has to pay the buyer dividends on the underlying stocks, as they become due. A contract of this nature will have a specified life, either of three months or of six months, after which it expires, i.e. is closed off. This allows for new baskets to be created which may be more representative of the particular index that is being tracked, because the 'old' basket will be likely to carry anomalies as a result of capitalizations or scrip issues. A basket, once created, cannot easily be adjusted, and so has to be run unchanged for the duration of the contract period.

Traded cash-baskets are not currently exchange-traded contracts, and this is regarded as one major drawback. Although they can be underwritten and cleared by triple A rated financial institutions, liquidity and trading visibility remains a handicap. They are also not really suitable for indices that comprise a large number of shares, like the FT-SE 100 Index. They are far more suitable for markets where portfolios of 5 to 20 equities can be used as a representative index, such as some of the smaller European or Scandinavian markets. Allowing for these limitations, cash-baskets do have certain attractions. One transaction gives the trader the ability to go long or short of the equivalent basket of shares without any worry about fair-value or basis risk that affects futures and options contracts. Time values, delta or gamma, do not have to be considered. Payment and collection of due dividends is arranged and guaranteed by the clearing house. Bid offer prices should be fairly tight or arbitrage opportunities will be seen between the quoted cash-basket prices and the underlying equities.

It is unlikely, though, that cash-baskets will ever make much impact in the derivative markets. Major institutions tend to be wary of non-exchange traded items; some are even forbidden to trade anything not quoted on a listed exchange by their corporate statutes. Futures markets provide liquidity, visibility of trading and the considerable advantage of dealing on a margin, thus allowing considerable gearing. Finally, with the universal availability of computers and 'basket software' at brokers' offices, institutional clients can demand quotations for large baskets of stock that they may wish either to purchase or sell. Such baskets will be unique to a particular investor and his investment strategy. It is the servicing of this 'bespoke' area, already very successful in the American markets, where more growth can be expected in Europe, rather than in the trading of specific but rigid bundles of equities.

Index participations—these are basically similar in concept to cash-baskets and are currently being developed mainly for the American market, although the London International Financial Futures Exchange has shown some interest in using similar contracts. They are 'evergreen' contracts linked to an underlying stock index and have an option to 'convert to cash' on a quarterly basis. Holders of long positions will, similarly to 'cash-baskets', receive a dividend; holders of short positions will be liable for these dividends.

Unlike cash-baskets, index participations (sometimes referred to as 'cash index participations') are expected to be traded on a margin basis, and not on a full payment of the total value. This, however, has proved to be a stumbling block as considerable debate has ensued between the Securities and Exchange Commission and the Commodity Futures Trading Commission as to who is responsible for regulating such a contract, and the degree of margin required, i.e. 5 per cent or 50 per cent. Until these factors are clarified, dividend bearing synthetic portfolios may not get past the planning stage in America. In any case they are unlikely to have as much general appeal as index futures or options contracts.

CHAPTER 9

Hedging

It is as well to remind ourselves that futures contracts developed initially for the sole purpose of providing producers and users of various commodities with an instrument that was able to 'hedge' financial risk. Producers of staple commodities, like the farmer growing wheat, can find it impossible to make any plans if he has no idea what price his crop will achieve whenever it is taken to market. With the introduction of futures contracts came the opportunity to hedge this uncertainty.

If the forward price is trading at a level where, if the farmer were to sell, he could guarantee for himself a comfortable return on his efforts, he can lock in this profit by selling a futures contract. On maturity of the crop, either this is delivered directly against the short futures position or more likely sold at the prevailing market price at the same time as unwinding the futures position—which will also reflect the prevailing market price. Thus, once a hedge position is established, further market movement is eliminated because what is lost on one position is gained on the other. The only risk remaining is that of basis risk, normally a very small risk element for someone looking to hedge market risk.

What our farmer has of course done, is to give up any hope of vast profits should it turn out that his particular crop is in great demand. On the other hand, if the market collapsed he would still be guaranteed his original profit. A prudent producer should not gamble and, in this instance, not using a futures or options strategy to protect oneself, is gambling.

Two interesting points arise which have analogies in other markets: firstly, the initial moment when a hedge position is opened is actually a speculation—if our farmer waited just a few minutes more, or a few more days, he might have locked himself into a much larger profit (or none at all). It is therefore sensible, particularly where it may be required to hedge a large position, not to attempt to put on the entire hedge at one point, but at several market levels. A range of trading positions is always more flexible than one position that is basically either right or wrong. Unwinding a hedge position will also be a speculation if the underlying is not liquidated (a wheat crop will be disposed of when the hedge is unwound, a portfolio of shares may still be in existence after a near-term market-risk hedge is taken off).

Secondly, it is often the farmer himself who will have the best idea as to whether his crop is developing well, whether the crops of all the other farmers are developing well, the chances of a glut, and the general pressure on prices over the coming seasons. Hedging is not just a purely technical application, even though there are systems available that take the discipline of risk management away from the individual and replace it by a computer programme. It still requires a large element of good fundamental analysis for it to be employed successfully.

Stock index contracts make it possible to manage investment exposure and control risk related to movements in equity markets through the use of hedging strategies. We must, however, be aware just what is possible to hedge, and what is not.

Total risk This is defined as:

total risk = systematic risk + non-systematic risk

The systematic risk is the market risk—the risk associated with the economy as a whole (Figure 9.1). These factors will affect all equities to some degree or other, factors such as changes in interest rates, political uncertainties, changes or perceived changes in fiscal policy, taxation and exchange rates.

Non-systematic risk, also known as specific risk, results from factors peculiar to a particular company. These are risks of technological development, technological achievements by competitors, labour relations, takeover situations and the cost of raw materials. These specific risks can only be reduced in a portfolio through increasing the breadth of investment. Systematic risk, on

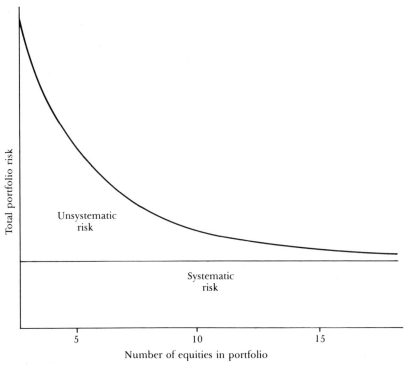

Figure 9.1   Total risk of a portfolio

the other hand, can be reduced and in some cases eliminated from a portfolio by hedging with index products.

Beta factors   Every equity is affected to a different degree by systematic risk. One particular piece of economic news, like a rise in interest rates, may be generally regarded as bad, but the effect on growth stocks will be more pronounced than on large cash-rich corporations that are well established in their own markets. Beta is a measure of this sensitivity to a change in an equities price in relation to the movement of the market as a whole, i.e. against the movement of the FT-SE 100, the CAC-40 or the S & P 500. An equity with a beta factor of 1.00 will move the same percentage up or down the market as a whole. An equity with a beta of 1.50 will on average move 1.5 per cent for each 1 per cent move in the market; a beta factor of 0.85 would indicate a stock that fluctuates less than that of the underlying market, i.e. 0.85 per cent for every 1 per cent market move.

Beta factors of equities are published by leading databases, and are calculated from a regression analysis of the equities against the market for a period of time. This emphasizes their handicap—beta factors can only be historical, and in the words of the industry's standard non-performance clause, historical performance is no guarantee of projected performance. It is, however, the best indicator that we have of how a moving market is likely to affect a particular equity, in effect it is the quantitative measure of market sensitivity.

Using the known beta factors of a portfolio of equities, it then becomes possible for a fund manager to work out a weighted arithmetic average beta factor for the portfolio itself. In a rising market a portfolio with a high beta (above 1.00) will rise faster than the market and so outperform the market. During a bear phase, a portfolio with a low beta will not lose as much money as the market average, and considerably less than a portfolio with a high beta. It therefore becomes possible for us to tune to the beta of a portfolio, either to create a more perfect hedge or to increase marginal performance when we have a strong market view.

EXAMPLE

We assume that a UK fund manager has an equity portfolio currently worth £10 million. The beta factor of the portfolio is 0.90, and because the fund manager expects the market to rise, he wants to increase the portfolio's beta to 0.95. He does this by buying a number of FT-SE 100 Index futures contracts. The number of contracts required can be calculated from the formula:

$$\frac{Vp\ (dB - aB)}{Vp}$$

where Vp is the value of the portfolio
dB is the desired beta
aB is the actual beta
Vp is the value of a futures contract

With the index at a level of 2450, the fund manager would therefore buy:

$$\frac{10\ 000\ 000 \times (0.95 - 0.90)}{2450 \times 25} = 8.16$$

or eight futures contracts.

Example

A fund manager with an equity portfolio worth £17 million and a beta factor of 1.18 expects the market to enter a short period of decline from its current level of 2600. To hedge the position and allow for the beta of the fund the manager needs to sell the following numbers of futures contracts:

$$\frac{17\,000\,000 \times 1.18}{2600 \times 25} = 308.6$$

Without the beta consideration only 261.5 contracts would have been opened.

R-squared   A portfolio is often described by its R^2 value. This is a statistical measure of the strength of the variation that can be attributed to the change in the index. It is also known as the coefficient of determination.

An R^2 of 0.95 will imply that 95 per cent of the change in price of a portfolio is due to changes in the overall market, i.e. systematic risk, the remaining 5 per cent movement is, therefore, as a result of specific risk. The closer the coefficient of determination is to one, the more confident we can be of our hedge performance. At the other end of the scale, R^2 ranges between one and zero, the portfolio would have no correlation with the market index, a theoretical 'portfolio' possibly comprising just one highly speculative penny share.

R^2 is directly related to the correlation coefficient, defined as the square root of the coefficient of determination. The correlation coefficient is positive if the beta is higher than one and negative if below one. Correlation analysis is a statistical technique used to measure the degree to which two variables move together; the techniques are the same whether we are comparing sales of ice-cream with the number of hours of sunshine, or the movement of a portfolio against a stock index. A correlation coefficient of 1, or 100 per cent indicates a perfect match between the two variables, a situation rarely, if ever, realized.

It is worth reminding ourselves that even if the coefficient of determination is one, for a portfolio relative to the stock index, the

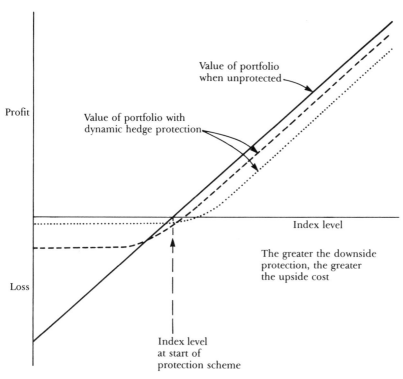

Figure 9.2 Desired aim of portfolio protection

beta of the portfolio may be quite different. The beta indicates how volatile the equity, or portfolio, is relative to the index, R^2, and the correlation coefficient tells us how good this relationship is.

General hedging strategies

In portfolio management, hedging is normally the initiation of a position in the stock index future or option contract that is intended as a convenient alternative to buying or selling large numbers of equities (Figure 9.2). The objectives may be quite diverse.

1. To reduce exposure to expected market weakness if holding a long stock position The fund manager expects the market to either go down or remain static for several months. The costs of selling a multi-plicity of stocks, only to buy them back some three months later are prohibitive not just from the point of view of dealing spreads and commissions. Other even more important considerations must be addressed. Selling large numbers of stocks is costly in effort and carries the risks that it may not be possible to buy back the required equities, at sensible prices, when the time is deemed to be right. This in turn will expose the fund manager to the risk of destroying the balance of a mature portfolio. By opening a short futures position, several advantages are gained. The mechanics of the trade are very quick and all dealing costs are substantially less (see page 55). Unwinding the short futures position once the expected market move has taken place, or after our own view has changed, is again just as simple. We can, if it suits us, run the futures position to its expiry, at which point the hedge will be unwound automatically. In addition, as we still retain our equity position, we are still receiving our full quota of dividends; and if the futures contract was sold at fair-value and either run to expiry or bought back at fair-value, then the finance costs of carrying the portfolio will also have been covered. This is a major advantage often overlooked: *A short futures position, opened and closed at fair-value, will carry the financing costs of maintaining a portfolio.*

However, this is dependent on fair-value or better being seen on the futures contract. Whenever hedging strategies are opened it must be remembered that *hedging substitutes basis risk for price risk.*

2. Elimination of systematic risk If we are fairly certain that our stock selection of a growth portfolio is good, but are uncertain of general market movement, we can open a futures short position thereby eliminating systematic risk and looking only for outperformance from the capital gains that will come from the growth stocks.

An extension of this would be to hedge only part of a portfolio. A fund manager may decide that only one sector was likely to perform well over the next quarter while everything else would go down. The answer here is to calculate the weighting of the part of the portfolio to be hedged, allow for its beta factor, and sell the correct number of futures contracts. Sector futures, such as the oil and gas index traded in the American Stock Exchange, could provide an even better solution to partial portfolio hedging. So far, although there have been attempts to develop such instruments, they have not been successful. This could be a 'future' area of growth, although liquidity on sector futures might be difficult to maintain in an official exchange. Possibly, OTC sector warrants developed by major integrated financial houses could be an attractive alternative.

It is also possible to hedge the systematic risk for one company only. An investor may be concerned that because the market is likely to fall, his ICI shares will also go down in value. He decides to hedge the risk by selling FT-SE 100 Index futures. With his holding worth £850 000 and the future trading at 2520 he has to sell

$$\frac{850\ 000}{2520 \times 25} = 13.5$$

An element of creativity might creep in here in that the fund manager now has to decide whether to sell 14 contracts and gear up on the hedge, or only sell 13 contracts and gear down. If the beta factor of ICI is taken into account (it is 0.98) it can then be demonstrated that only 13.2 contracts are required for the hedge, so 13 would be nearest to the theoretical requirement. While beta factors on very small portfolios of less than £1 million will only have a very marginal effect, the success of the hedge will, nevertheless, depend on the same factors applicable to much larger portfolios (namely, how the basis changes between the opening and the closing of the hedge, and the strength of the beta relationship between its historical and current performance).

Aggressive stock selection funds can use futures to completely hedge out the systematic risk of every stock purchased, thereby creating a fund that should considerably outperform the market average during bear phases. In bull markets, such positions need to be unwound through the use of dynamic hedging disciplines.

3. To fix portfolio value in anticipation of future sale

Example

Index level today is 2680; future at 2730. The value of the equity portfolio today is £120 million. The equity portfolio is to be liquidated in two months but the interim market view is very bearish.

$$\text{action: sell } \frac{120\ 000\ 000}{25 \times 2730} = 1758 \text{ futures contracts}$$

Two months later the market and futures contract is at 2580. Close futures and liquidate equities.

$$\text{loss on equities} = 120\,000\,000 \left(\frac{1 - 2580}{2680}\right)$$
$$= £4\,477\,620$$

$$\text{gain on future} = (2730 - 2580) \times 25 \times 1758$$
$$= £6\,592\,500$$

The strategy results in a net gain of £2 114 880 over and above the hedge requirement, and arises from the fact that when the position was opened the futures contract was trading at a premium to the underlying market. If this premium was at fair-value then the 'gain' should equate to the financing costs of the portfolio—a welcome addition to the initial hedge requirement.

Such a strategy can be used whenever the market has risen to a particularly attractive level that a fund manager believes cannot be sustained, and he expects to have to sell stock several months hence when prices may not be attractive. A short futures position is opened on the index. When the time comes for the equity position to be liquidated, the futures contracts are bought back, hopefully showing the profit that would have occurred if the equities had been sold earlier.

4. To fix the price on an anticipated stock purchase As a converse to the previous strategy, should the market appear at very attractive levels, a fund manager can 'buy-the-market' via a stock index futures contract in anticipation of receiving investment funds. When the expected funds arrive, stock selection can be made at a leisurely pace and the index futures sold at the same rate as stock investments are made. Because of the large gearing effect we only need to put up a fraction of the underlying value, as margin. The cash position does, however, have to be liquid enough to allow for additional variation margin should the near-term market movement be adverse to our futures position.

5. To reduce underexposure in a fluctuating market This is an extension of our previous strategy except that here we are in a position where funds are available, although at present not fully invested. If the market is now perceived to be much more attractive, rapid exposure can be gained through buying the stock index futures contract. One can then make unhurried use of available research in order to decide which particular sector and equities one should buy, and as this is done, so to reduce market exposure in the index future.

6. *Hedging the systematic risk of unit trusts* If a unit trust manager finds that more units have been encashed than sold, and he is now holding a large number of units in his 'box', he has the choice of several actions. One is to break the units up and sell off the underlying equities; this will involve dealing costs, may be very cumbersome if a large number of equities are involved, may upset the balance of the unit trust if all equities are not sold, and will involve all these problems in reverse order if suddenly more units are sold than encashed. The unit trust manager can decide to do nothing, thereby accepting the risk that the market could move against the units which then might have to be sold at a loss.

An elegant solution from many points of view is to hedge this risk by selling futures contracts to the underlying value of the units held in the unit trust manager's box. Ideally, the market risk is removed; in addition, the cost of financing the equities is covered by the basis, and the manager can concentrate his or her efforts on marketing the units and taking out a risk-free 5 per cent round turn. In practice, the results may not be quite as perfect. Basis risk has to be considered, although over a long period this should even out. A more significant problem is that it may actually not be possible to hedge more than part of the risk of the unit trust.

A unit trust designed to track the CAC-40 or FT-SE 100 Index will not give us any problem. A unit trust designed to provide income from blue-chip companies, together with some growth, will still be fairly easy to hedge as the beta factor of the fund should be reasonably constant. Even funds based on particular sectors of the economy will have a large element of systematic risk that can be hedged. Problems come with 'recovery' trust, 'special situation' trusts and exotics like 'pan-European-growth-and-gold-fund'. While in each of these funds there will be a degree of systematic risk, even if it is multinational and snapshot beta factors can be calculated, any hedge should never be regarded as anything more than a very partial cover. Growth funds will in any case tend to concentrate their investments in companies that are young and so their betas have little track record, or companies which because of

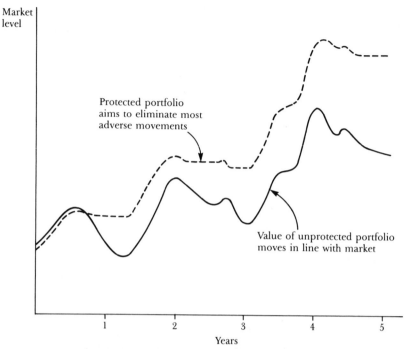

Figure 9.3 Theoretical aim of portfolio protection

'special situations' have changing beta values. Companies will show reducing betas as they grow and mature.

For these more 'difficult to hedge' unit trusts the R-squared factor can be an additional useful guide to portfolio performance. We are, nevertheless, not going to be able to design an ideal hedge for every different unit trust. Where a particular institutional investment group has several unit trusts under management, there is the opportunity to hedge the 'box' of 'boxes'. Under such an arrangement there is likely to be a better hedge correlation, as the sum will tend to be near the characteristics of the index. The tradeoff may be an internal administrative nightmare!

7. Portfolio Insurance This takes many forms and the term itself has come to mean different things to different people (Figure 9.3). The essence, however, is still the same in that portfolio insurance seeks to insure that if the market declines, the value of the portfolio will be maintained; if the market rises, the comparable rise in the value of the portfolio will be achieved. If this sounds like an ideal world then it is worth remembering that insurance costs money, the better the insurance the more it costs, and no one will insure against 'acts of God', equivalent approximately to an overnight market collapse of 15 per cent. These constraints notwithstanding, portfolio insurance is an area worth exploring.

(i) Buying index puts—the most straightforward form of protection The cost of the insurance is determined by the premium paid, so is a known factor. Disadvantages are that if we attempted to deal in far forward months, market liquidity may not be great enough to absorb large positions without moving the market against us. Also if we expect to maintain an insurance position for any length of time we cannot assess in advance the costs of rolling positions. Using index put warrants instead of options may resolve some of these problems. Using this strategy, if the market rises we gain the benefit of the portfolio increasing in value in line with the market once the insurance premium—the cost of the puts or warrants— has been covered. If the market falls, the portfolio is 'covered' below the strike price of the option or warrant, less the cost of the puts. The higher the strike price that we seek to protect, the higher the premium.

(ii) Writing index calls This strictly speaking is not a full hedge in that the protection obtained is equivalent only to the premium received. If the market declines to the level where this protection is exhausted, new index calls can be written. This does, however, start to become a rather dangerous strategy because if the market rallies strongly the calls will be exercised and the call writer, in this case the portfolio insurer, will bear an opportunity cost. Writing more calls before the old ones have expired will also expose one to double gearing if the market rallies strongly (above the highest strike price).

(iii) Buying puts on individual stocks This gives an advantage that one can select vulnerable stocks and only hedge those. On the negative side, our stock selection has to be good, premiums are generally higher than for the index, and not every stock has a put listed on the market. This strategy is chiefly of interest in portfolios holding a small number of blue-chip stocks.

(iv) Selling futures contracts at predetermined levels Over the last 15 years much work has been done on developing techniques that will

protect a fund through the use of dynamic hedging. Basically, as
the market is rising and protection is needed less and less, fewer
short positions are held; as the market declines numbers of short
futures contracts are increased, thereby increasing the size of the
hedge. A dynamic approach to hedging like this does have considerable problems if a market oscillates between certain levels,
triggering hedging action, and then with changing direction causing the hedge subsequently to be unwound. A market action of this
nature causes the dynamic hedger to 'buy high' and 'sell low',
consistently locking in small losses. This, however, is no different
to buying puts and watching the market either stagnate or oscillate
around the strike level. Both strategies here involve a cost. The
portfolio insurance strategies start to come into their own when the
market starts to trend, and like almost all other investment
'techniques of success', the great trick is to be on the right side of a
major trend. The aim of our dynamic hedging programme is to do
just that.

In slightly greater detail, the system works as follows. A portfolio
manager, believing that the market is rather high takes a decision
to open a hedge position equivalent to 40 per cent of the underlying
value of his fund. If the market now falls and the value of the
portfolio declines, 40 per cent of the portfolio will be protected.
The fund manager will have decided on his strategy beforehand,
and at a particular point, say when the market has declined 3 per
cent from his original level, he will increase his futures short
position by a further 20 per cent of the value of the fund. The
hedge now accounts for 60 per cent of the fund. If the market still
falls further, the short position will be providing increasing profits
to offset the losses on the equity positions of the portfolio. If we
maintain the strategy that we started, a decline of a further 6 per
cent in the market will see our fund manager fully insured against
further losses in a declining market. As we are running a short
futures position and can expect to have sold futures at a premium
to the cash market (ideally at fair-value or above), the futures
position will be producing an interest rate return equivalent to
financing our hedged stock.

At some point our well-behaved downward trend will run out of
sellers and a new bull phase will start. The fund manager now has
to decide on his particular strategy. To unwind the short hedge
positions at the same index levels as they were opened will simply

result in us being exactly where we started once the market has recovered 12 per cent (but having gained a financing contribution via the short future).

If the market has bounced from a new low, moving averages as well as other technical indicators are generating 'buy' signals, and fundamentals are improving, the bold fund manager may decide to unwind his entire hedge position and cash-in. Unfortunately, no one can ever be certain that the market has peaked or bottomed; sadly no one rings a bell or blows a whistle at these important points. Cashing-in on entire hedge position, in retrospect can often turn out to have been badly timed. On the other hand, it is certainly preferable to the earlier scenario of unwinding hedges at the same levels as they were opened. If a total hedge has been unwound, but the expected market recovery fails to manifest itself, a new hedging programme can be started. At any event, the dynamic hedger will be far better off than the fund manager who just sat and watched the value of his portfolio decline. Once it is decided to buy back futures contracts as the market rises, they should be bought back either at lower levels than they were sold, or at a faster rate.

In the case where the original hedge position was proved incorrect one should buy back the short futures on predetermined market rises, and then let the market take the unhedged portfolios upwards until the fund manager decides that it is again right to start a new portfolio insurance programme. This will be caused by a change in a fundamental view, a technical trigger, like a moving average cross-over, or a 3 per cent setback from a new high.

The parameters that one can develop, and have been developed by various participants in this field, can become highly sophisticated. The problems of when to start a portfolio insurance hedge, for how long it should last, and to what index levels, tend to be straightfoward decisions that the fund manager inputs. However, the more difficult ones address the problems of basis risk whenever using futures, the extent to which the fund deviates from its beta value and hence the correlation of the hedge, and the increased costs of dealing that have to be borne in the instance that a sudden increase in volatility causes a whip-saw effect (buying expensive futures and then selling them cheaply).

Even with all these points resolved to the satisfaction of the fund manager, the new more volatile age of investment since the events of October 1987 does mean that one is for ever glancing over one's shoulder. What will happen if in the morning the market opens 12 per cent lower? Aside from several obvious answers, it will mean that an orderly portfolio insurance scheme will have been poleaxed by volatility. However, this should not put off potential users of insurance techniques. Extreme market movements are very rare, and usually do not come totally out of the blue (bull markets can cope with large amounts of bad news before they start to turn down, a bear market may only need one more small bit of bad news to cause a collapse of confidence), so indications will already be apparent that demonstrate a change of trend and thus the need for a new hedge strategy. The experience of several funds actively using portfolio insurance in the UK during the time of the October 1987 crash gave a consensus view that while each individual system broke down in some way—mainly through not being able to achieve adequate hedge cover at the right index levels—all the funds had some degree of hedge cover before the crash, putting them far better off than any of their competitors who had none.

Portfolio insurance strategies, as opposed to straightforward hedging will not appeal to everyone, but there are certain types of fund that might find it worth considering. Examples include funds that are particularly sensitive to market declines, such as pension funds that do not have large reserves, and new investment schemes that have little track record and are prepared to sacrifice some performance in order to ensure no large losses.

Hedging summary

Futures contracts evolved as a result of the need to manage risk. As equity values, and consequently portfolio values, fluctuate in response to systematic and non-systematic effects, stock index futures and stock index warrants and options can be used to control systematic risks. As the basic hedging strategy involves equal and opposite positions between equity and futures positions (i.e. long of stock and short of stock index futures), hedged positions will ensure that what is lost on one position is gained on the other. Possible systematic gains are foregone in order to avoid systematic losses. However, few hedges are perfect and the risks that the hedger must be aware of are those of basis and beta.

In all instances we are using futures and options because these instruments are far cheaper and quicker to use than dealings in the underlying equities themselves. These factors lead us naturally to consider using index futures in dynamic hedging strategies. No longer do we have to be 'passive' with our hedge. We can develop strategies that will enable us to protect all or part of our portfolio from adverse moves. We can decide on the level that we wish to protect and the period of time we want the 'insurance' to last. Dynamic hedging can be tailored to what a particular portfolio needs within the constraints of dealing and volatility costs.

Table 9.1 Hedging strategies

Objectives	Action
1. Reduce exposure of long position	Sell futures Buy put options or warrants Sell call options (limited use)
2. Reduce effect of short position	Buy futures Buy call options or warrants Sell put options (limited use)
3. Fixing portfolio value in the short term	Sell futures
4. Fixing level of intended portfolio purchase	Buy futures
5. Protecting value of portfolio below particular levels	Sell futures on market declines once 'trigger' levels achieved

CHAPTER 10

International opportunities

The continuing growth of multinational corporations and the reduction of cross-border investment controls has naturally led to a flourishing international investment market. Additionally, the high visibility and profile given to overseas markets through their own indices now means that we can instantly compare investment returns from one country to the next, even after allowing for variations in exchange rates.

As institutional fund managers find themselves being ranked and compared more and more against their competitors, a disproportionate degree of importance is now attached to short-term investment performance. Consequently, no one can afford to be ignorant of a surging stock market outside their own domestic sphere. If a particular overseas market is growing at 20 per cent while the domestic market is showing gains of only 5 per cent, questions would rightly be asked if more funds were not transferred to the country of significantly better returns. Modern technology allows fund managers to keep an eye on almost any corner of the world that they wish, while the large investment and securities houses also have the international involvement to allow them to undertake in depth research of overseas economies as well as of particular overseas equities. Despite these factors, the volume of overseas investment when compared to domestic investment is very small for most countries. Aside from the one spectacular example, Hong Kong, which has over 60 per cent of its private sector pension assets invested outside Hong Kong, most other countries are covered by the 0 per cent to 20 per cent overseas investment band, with the bias below 10 per cent. This area of cross-border investment is therefore one that could see considerable growth in the coming decade.

Several serious problems remain, suggesting that although trading in cross-border equities will increase, trading in overseas index derivatives may actually be the preferred vehicle of investment.

Firstly, although trading index derivative requires a certain degree of sophistication, it is easier to master the art of investment via index products than to be aware of all the factors affecting a basket of physical equities. It is also cheaper to utilize the services of one competent index specialist (who can then trade in any part of the world) rather than many separate specialist stock selectors.

Secondly, liquidity of overseas stocks can be limited. It is sometimes quite difficult to determine the liquidity of stocks in one's own domestic market—obtaining accurate information on unfamiliar overseas equities can be quite daunting. The investor can all too easily discover that getting into an active overseas equity presents no difficulty; getting out of an inactive foreign stock may be almost impossible.

Lastly, the processing of international equity trades can be protracted, complex and consequently costly. Because so many different parties are involved, investors, brokers, overseas brokers, banks and clearing systems, much can go wrong—even though action is being taken to unify international dealing and clearing techniques.

For these reasons it seems reasonable to expect a substantial degree of international trading to develop via the derivatives markets at a faster rate than through equities. We have already seen in Chapter 8 how assets may be moved from one country to another by the use of synthetic index funds, a combination of stock index, futures contracts and interest-bearing securities. Exposure to one country can very quickly be increased, exposure to another can be terminated or indeed made negative. Most global investment, however, is contained in what are now seen as three major industrial blocks, namely, the USA, Japan and SE Asia, and Europe. While it has been a straightforward operation to increase or decrease investment in the USA, via several stock index contracts, chiefly the S & P 500, and in Japan either through TOPIX or the Nikkei Index, Europe has for some time been a far more complex investment problem.

Europe and its indices

With the development of an ever more integrated Europe, overseas investors, particularly those from the USA and Japan, are starting to regard 'Europe' as more of a single investment area. In many places the old belief that the European market meant the UK, Germany and France, with a few significant corporations in some of the other countries, still holds. The reasons are not difficult to find. Attempting to invest in 15 different countries via 15 differing stock markets, with more or less 15 differing currencies, not to mention 10 possible languages, can be daunting to say the least. With the advent of stock index futures contracts in the UK, France and then Germany, investors can now develop synthetic funds that cover approximately 65 per cent of the capitalization of Europe. To cover the greater part of the remaining 35 per cent requires considerably more effort as today futures or options are still not available in all European countries.

To satisfy the need for a totally European product the London International Financial Futures Exchange launched two European index products.

FT-SE Eurotrack 100

This index was introduced by the International Stock Exchange in London in October 1990, and is a capitalization-weighted index made up of 100 continental European stocks, i.e. Europe without the UK.

The index is calculated each minute from 0945 to 1530, converted to Deutschmarks and like the FT-SE 100 Index, is monitored on at least a quarterly basis to determine whether companies should be dropped from the index in order to make way for suitable better candidates. A reserve list of possible new contenders is also published.

When this index was first proposed, there was a considerable degree of debate as to whether it should not be an index that included the UK and so would thus be a really European index. The view, however, prevailed that particularly as this index was aimed at giving UK investors a view of how continental Europe was performing, the UK element did not have to be included. There was also a strong lobby from some UK fund managers that as a futures contract was already available on the UK market, in order to fill the derivative hole, all that was needed was the ability to trade the non UK 'bit', and all would be well. This might be a reasonable view taken from an isolated 'island' perspective, but still causes considerable bewilderment to American, Japanese and continental European investors who are starting to view Europe more and more as a single area of investment rather than a dozen fragmented ones. By way of stemming such criticisms, as Eurotrack 100 was being launched the International Stock Exchange also announced that Eurotrack 200, an all-European index, would be launched in 1991.

For the UK investor looking at continental Europe, however, Eurotrack 100 is a very useful tool and has a close correlation with other recognized European 'benchmark' indices. Back calculation over a five-year period between 31 December 1985 and the 31 December 1990, when compared to the FT-Actuaries World Indices and the Morgan Stanley Capital International Indices for Europe excluding the UK, gave the results shown in Table 10.1.

Interestingly, the French and German sectors of Eurotrack 100 also track the CAC-40 and DAX very closely over the same three-year period, with a correlation of 0.999 to the CAC-40 and 0.995 to the DAX.

With these correlations the Eurotrack should be acceptable as another 'benchmark' index, which also has the advantage of being traded on the derivatives market. Its acceptance to a large extent will depend both on the success of the derivative products that grow from it and to a lesser extent on the degree of future correlation with the other recognized indices. All too often an index has been rigorously back tested and shown to give a very high degree of correlation with a recognized base, only to develop an action all of its own once it becomes live and starts to be used for trading.

The futures contract on the FT-SE Eurotrack 100

This was introduced in June 1991 in order to provide investors with a means of trading 'Continental Europe'. The contract is traded by open outcry on the LIFFE and is priced in DM, a natural choice of currency as the index itself is calculated in DM, and Germany accounts for the largest weighting. Contract size is

Table 10.1   FT-SE Eurotrack 100 tracking performance (DM)

Index	Correlation	Mean monthly difference %	Monthly error %
FT-AWI Europe Ex UK	0.993	0.03	0.69
MSCI Europe Ex UK	0.993	0.03	0.71
MSCI Europe Ex UK (FREE)	0.993	0.15	0.61
Broad Market Index Ex UK	0.995	0.04	0.59
Primary Market Index Ex UK	0.996	0.06	0.49

Source: 'FT-SE Share Indices', London Stock Exchange, London, 1991

	Country weightings April 1991	
	FT-SE Eurotrack 100	*FT-AWI Europe Ex UK*
Germany	26%	26%
France	22%	22%
Netherlands	13%	11%
Italy	10%	10%
Switzerland	11%	9%
Spain	7%	8%
Belgium	5%	5%
Sweden	4%	3%
Others	2%	6%

Source: 'Eurotrack', LIFFE, London 1991

DM 100 per index point, and minimum price movement is half an index point (full details are given in Appendix 2).

The last trading day of the FT-SE Eurotrack 100 is the third Friday of the delivery month. For investors who wish to use both the FT-SE 100 and the Eurotrack 100 as a means of gaining total European exposure, allowance has to be made for these different expiry times. Also the exchange has done its best to avoid contract expiry on any of the 10 business days each year when the index is quoted 'part'. These are days when less than 75 per cent of the capitalization of the Eurotrack 100 Index is available as a result of continental European public holidays. Under such circumstances the unwinding of arbitrage positions may be hampered. While official holidays are predictable, with the diversity of Europe there are always possibilities that the index may suddenly become 'part' quoted as a result of a particular difficulty in some part of Europe (power failure, national emergency, market suspension or special holiday). These factors cannot be allowed for.

Further and more serious complexities that have to be addressed when considering pan-national indices are fair-value and currency.

Fair-value is calculated in the same manner as described in Chapter 3, but with the added complication that the calculation is made up of 11 parts (countries) with their own individual finance rates and dividend payment characteristics. For the purposes of some simplicity certain assumptions have to be made: no transaction costs, dividends are known, tax implications can be ignored, settlement dates are uniform, margin requirements can be ignored and interest rates are the same for all participants. These same assumptions are made when calculating the FT-SE 100 Index fair-value, and most other index fair-values. However, as we are dealing with a 'complex' index, such assumptions can compound any errors. It is, therefore, no surprise that a dozen different participants all calculating fair-value for Eurotrack may end up with a dozen different (but hopefully close) figures.

Normally one expects fair-value to show the futures contract at a premium to the cash index because dividends paid are lower than the costs of financing. For Eurotrack 100 this is not always so. Because about 75 per cent of dividends generated by Eurotrack in a year are paid during the months of May, June and July, it is possible that at certain times during this period fair-value can be negative, i.e. the future should be at a discount to the cash index (Figure 10.1).

The currency factor of Eurotrack 100 arises because the constituent domestic stocks have to be converted to a DM price. While this extra calculation only marginally complicates the algorithm used to generate the final index, from an investment viewpoint a new factor must be considered. In an extreme case, the stock markets of the constituent countries may not be moving at all while the comprehensive index could be displaying substantial volatility. The index is not just a stock index, it is also affected by currency movements.

Creating a synthetic pan-European fund

In order to attain a pan-European weighting the FT-A currently indicate an investment of 58 per cent in Europe without the UK,

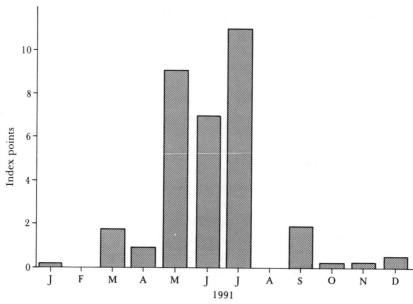

Figure 10.1 Dividend payments for FT-SE Eurotrack 100 Index
1991

and an investment of 42 per cent in the UK. To achieve this using FT-SE futures and Eurotrack futures would require the following numbers of respective contracts:

FT-SE 100 futures contract value =
contract size × index level × DM exchange rate =
£25 × 2650 × 2.9 = DM 192 125

FT-SE Eurotrack futures contract value =
Contract size × index level =
DM 100 × 1180 = DM 118 000

To achieve a 58/42 weighting we need

1 FT-SE contract to $\dfrac{58}{42} \times \dfrac{192\,125}{118\,000}$ Eurotrack

= 1 FT-SE to 2.248 Eurotrack contracts
or 100 FT-SE contract for every 225 Eurotrack

For a fully synthetic European index fund, the underlying futures value would have to be placed on deposit, the Eurotrack element on DM deposit and the UK element on sterling deposit. Weightings may subsequently have to be adjusted if currencies move out of line.

Eurotop 100 Index

Almost at the same time as LIFFE started to trade the Eurotrack 100, the Financial Futures Market Amsterdam introduced a contract on their Eurotop 100 Index. Unlike Eurotrack, Eurotop is a pan-European index made up of 100 of the largest and most liquid stocks from 9 countries; 22 from the UK, Germany and France with 15 each, Switzerland and Italy with 10 each, The Netherlands, Spain and Sweden with 8, and Belgium represented with 4 stocks. The index is recalculated every 15 seconds of the trading day in ECUs. The numbers of stocks used in each country equate to the percentage relative weightings of each country and are derived from exchange capitalizations and GNPs. Like Eurotrack, Eurotop also has an options contract in addition to the futures contract.

Although interest in these European indices has been considerable, actual trading volumes have initially been disappointing. Institutional investors are only slowly starting to look at them. Whether the broader, but ex-UK, Eurotrack priced in DM is more acceptable than the pan-European Eurotop priced in ECU, but with its reduced ability to track the constituent countries, is a better or worse trading vehicle still remains to be seen. A disadvantage of both of these contracts is the sheer difficulty of arbitraging between the contracts and the underlying equities. This automatically removes the constraints that would tend to force the future to trade within arbitrageable levels either side of fair-value, as well as severely reducing trading volumes and open interest. However, as a means of increasing or decreasing European investment exposure in a global context, or just taking a speculative view of the 'European economy', these instruments may yet find a significant role.*

Eurotrack 200

The International Stock Exchange in London launched this 'pan-European index' on 25 February 1991 to provide a means of tracking the performance of the leading equities in Europe. Unfortunately, it is not a simple capitalization-weighted index of the top 200 companies in Europe, but an amalgam of the FT-SE 100 Index

---

* From September 1992, LIFFE has suspended the Eurotrack futures and options contracts because of poor trading volumes.

of the UK and the non-UK FT-SE Eurotrack 100. As these two indices were already in existence, it was far easier to combine the two than to start a new index from scratch.

Because a simple amalgamation of the two indices would give excessive weighting to the UK, the effect of the FT-SE 100 is restrained by a 'weighting restraint factor'. This weighting restraint factor is equal to the proportion of the weighting of the UK against that of Continental Europe, this gives us an index that to all intents and purposes is a capitalization-weighted European index. However, with the larger UK sample it can be argued that the Continental European element might not be so accurately computed and give rise to tracking errors against any larger Continental European sample.

These considerations by themselves illustrate the sheer difficulty of providing a representative real-time index. Other 'passive' indices that are calculated daily on the basis of closing prices are certainly better guides as to how markets are moving, but of no use as the underlying instrument of trade. The Eurotrack 200 Index is calculated every minute from 0945 to 1530 London time and the published 'price' is converted to ECU.

The Index Administration Committee has made provision for quarterly meetings which review the selection of stocks as well as the index weighting restraint factor. Because of the large number of sources of information needed to keep the index updated, there are likely to be times when some stock exchanges may not be able to function properly. Should at any time there be less than 75 per cent of the index constituents by capitalization with firm prices (this is also to allow for national holidays), the index is indicated as being based on a 'partial' calculation. A major system problem causes the index to be declared 'indicative'.

FT-Actuaries Indices

In the UK market the major compiler of various equity indices is the *Financial Times* in association with the Institute of Actuaries and the Faculty of Actuaries. As well as compiling indices representing the whole market, there are also available a very large number of component indices that relate to particular sectors of the equity market.

The FT-Actuaries All Share Index

This for the UK is still seen as the most accurate measure of the performance of the equity market and is used as the yardstick against which investment funds are judged. Even investments that have no pretentions about being an index tracking fund will still be compared to the FT All Share to see whether they are under or over-performing against the standard. The main reason why the All Share is so used is that, as it is made up of over 710 underlying equities, it has a broad coverage of the UK market. It represents just over 80 per cent of the total capitalization of the UK market, and as it is calculated on a capitalization-weighted arithmetic basis, it will behave in line with a portfolio.

Because of the large number of equities used, the various component sectors are also represented in considerable depth, and this allows the FT All Share to be broken down into its 40 component sector indices. These can then be used to analyse which particular sectors are performing better than others and how specific equities are moving against either the whole market or their own sector.

Because of the diversity of the All Share Index, constant monitoring is required of the constituents to make sure that they still have adequate weightings and are representative of their sector. Changes are frequent. Takeovers, mergers, growth of new companies together with the occasional bankruptcy ensure that the index has to be updated constantly. As markets develop there may be the need to develop entirely new sectors or to liquidate outdated ones.

Originally, all the component sectors of the All Share started at a level of 100 in 1962; today it is interesting to see how much disparity has crept into the various sectors and how badly some sectors, like 'mechanical engineering', have done compared to 'leisure'.

The FT-Actuaries World Index

With the progressive globalization of equities, it is now important to be able to have a view on the general state of the world's equity market. This gives both a general view on whether global prices are rising or falling and information about the relative performance of any particular part of the world.

The FT-Actuaries World Index was introduced in March 1987, specifically to meet these newly developing needs and possibly to be used as the global benchmark by investors as well as the underlying index for new derivative products. It is based on nearly 2500 equities (selected from a global total of over 15 000) from 24 countries. These equities represent approximately 70 per cent of the total market capitalization of the world's major stock exchanges, but the equities selected must be available for international investment. The index is calculated at the end of the day, once the New York market has closed, and is published in three currencies, the US$, sterling and the local domestic currency. It is a capitalization-weighted arithmetic average with adjustments as necessary for capitalization changes.

With about 2500 equities to monitor on a daily basis just to calculate the index, and also the need to watch the reserve lists in case constituent changes have to be made, the operation is broken down between several 'managers'. Broadly, the *Financial Times* looks after Europe, Goldman Sachs takes care of North America and Mexico and the Pacific Basin region is monitored by County Natwest Securities.

The index, as mentioned, seeks to cover 70 per cent of global equity capitalization and this in turn is projected to cover, where possible, 70 per cent of the underlying national markets. Exceptions come where there are restrictions on international trading of equities, or where particular but otherwise suitable companies have large single holdings that may inhibit their liquidity. Selection to the index is not solely on the basis of capitalization, but also on representative suitability.

Like the FT All Share Index, the World Index is also broken down into constituents, in this case 11 regional indices, 36 composite industry indices as well as over 100 sub-industry categories— all useful benchmarks for assessing performance on an international scale.

Other global indices

Although the FT-Actuaries World Index has a high profile in the UK because of its association with the Financial Times, it is not the only global index in existence. Others should also be considered.

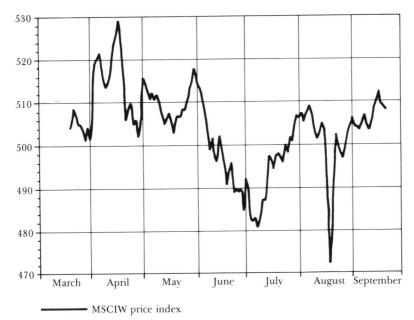

Figure 10.2 The global view—MSCIW Index for March to
September 1991

Source: Datastream plc, 1991. Reproduced with permission

1. The Morgan Stanley Capital International World Index (MSCIW)

This index actually has the oldest pedigree and was established in
the 1960s. Morgan Stanley bought the index from Capital Group,
an independent Los Angeles based investment management organization. For many fund managers this particular index is the norm
that they use when comparing investment performance on a global
scale (Figure 10.2).

The MSCIW Index aims to track 60 per cent of global capitalization using approximately 1400 constituents taken from 19 different international stock exchanges. It is also quoted daily in the
Financial Times.

2. Salomon-Russel Global Equity Index.

This is produced from the joint efforts of Salomon Brothers and
the Frank Russel Company—an American pension fund consulta-
tive group.

3. The Euromoney/First Boston Global Stock Index

This is produced by collaboration between a team at First Boston, and published monthly by *Euromoney*. It is calculated from almost 1300 equities in 17 different markets. The total number of equities used is about 1600 taken from 24 countries. With 1000 of the 1600 equities being American, this index is rather less representative of the rest of the world.

This list of international stock indices is by no means complete, more are still appearing. One of the problems of index acceptance was illustrated when Morgan Stanley purchased the Capital International series of indices. Rival investment banks decided they could no longer use an index with a Morgan Stanley name by which to judge their own performance, so either sought other indices or developed their own. Rivalry between indices has also been seen in Switzerland and Germany where different banks created their own indices and then battled for supremacy. An index appears to be more acceptable to investors if the index creator is not associated with a financial institution but rather an independent body or publishing house such as the Standard & Poor's or *Financial Times*. Acceptance of an index is also dependent on the degree to which it actually represents what the investor can achieve. There is little point in comparing the performance of a real fund with a theoretical index, if significant numbers of the equities included cannot be purchased or readily traded in the international market place. Companies with large family or limited investor holdings, countries that do not have a fully accessible stock market, or many crossed shareholdings between companies (like Japanese banks) are all factors that make it very difficult if not impossible to accumulate sufficient stock to give a correct weighting to a 'global index tracking fund'.

These difficulties notwithstanding, international investment in equities continues to grow, and with this the need for indexation, but whether any particular index becomes the dominant one still remains to be seen.

Dominance of the international stock indexation business will also lead to the launch of derivative products, and since 1988 several contenders have registered their intention to produce a global index futures contract. Experience has, however, shown that a futures contract is unlikely to succeed if it does not have a strong underlying physical market—here one can agree that while the underlying market exists, it is still not 'tangible' enough for the needs of international investors. It may not be so difficult for a capable investor to take a reasonably good view of his own market for the purposes of a speculative investment, quite another to catch the pulse of the global economy. Arbitrageurs are also likely to be daunted by the complexity of buying representative stock, in order to lock in a profit against an expensive sale of futures. Global shorting of stock in order to open a short stock-long futures position may in fact prove to be impossible.

Trading volume for global stock index futures contracts if they do finally get off the ground is likely to come from investors using the contract in order either to develop fully synthetic global index funds or part synthetic global index funds. Short positions may be employed by those looking for hedge protection, both dynamic or static.

With such trading possibilities in mind, several global indices have been registered as possible contenders for a futures contract: an International Market Index is planned to be traded on the CSCE; the New York Futures Exchange has sponsored the Global Analysis System 100 International Index (GAS); and for possible trading on the CME, a partial global index, the Morgan Stanley Capital International Europe, Australia and Far East Index, or the EAFE.

The early euphoria has subsided a little since the early work was done on possible global indices. Problems of calculation, trading by either a screen-based or open outcry system as well as settlement procedures, have in the main been resolved. What still holds back final development is the risk that the time may still not be right. The bear market that has followed the crash of 1987 has been a difficult time to launch new index products, and with a global index product the risk of failure is more severe, a failure would be visible on a global scale. Caution in the launch of such an instrument is understandable.

From a different perspective, a global index futures contract may actually have very little extra to offer from that which is available already. Investors generally have adequate exposure to their own domestic markets, but have a problem in making adequate investments in other countries. An American fund may find that by using a global futures contract to create a synthetic index fund, one is actually doubling up on one's domestic exposure. The answer to the creation of a global synthetic index fund may well lie in the use of combinations of already existent indices, similar to Eurotrack 200 being an amalgam of the FT-SE 100 and Eurotrack 100.

By using the S & P 500, Topix, and Eurotrack 200 an investor is already gaining exposure to 85 per cent of global weighting and, for many investors, almost 100 per cent of the required global spread. To complete the global exposure only small adjustments may be needed to include Australia, South East Asia and possibly South America and South Africa.

By using such a global approach to synthetic investment funds, switching from one part of the world to another or changing asset allocations is quite straightforward.

Listing of details of stock index futures and options contracts

While every attempt has been made to make the following list as up to date as possible, changes are constantly being made to contracts by their parent exchanges. Some contracts may disappear altogether, many new ones are likely to appear over the next few years. Traders wishing to deal should in all cases check latest contract details with the responsible exchanges.

Australia

Contract   Twenty Leaders Index Future
Exchange   ASX Futures Market
Contract size   Index × A$100
Minimum price move (value)   0.1 (A$10)
Settlement   Two days after expiry
Trading months   Nearest four months
Trading hours   1000–1600
Expiry   Last business day of expiry month

Australia

Contract   Australian Stock Exchange All Ordinaries Share Price
  Index Future
Exchange   Sydney Futures Exchange
Contract size   Index × A$100
Minimum price move (value)   0.1 (A$10)
Settlement   On second day following last trade day
Trading months   March, June, September, December

Trading hours   0930–1230, 1400–1610
Expiry   1610 on last business day of contract month

Australia

Contract   All Ordinaries Share Price Index Option
Exchange   Sydney Futures Exchange
Contract size   Index × A$100
Minimum price move   0.1
Settlement   One futures contract
Trading months   March, June, September, December
Trading hours   0930–1230, 1400–1610
Expiry   Last business day of contract month
Style   American

Belgium

Contract   Belgian Stock Index Future
Exchange   BELFOX Brussels
Contract size   Index × BF100
Minimum price move (value)   0.01 (BF1.0)
Settlement   On expiry
Trading months   Nearest three months plus March, June,
   September, December cycle
Trading hours   1015–1600
Last trading day   Seven business days before end of contract
   month

Brazil

Contract   IBOVESPA Stock Index Future
Exchange   Bolsa Brasileira de Futuros, Rio de Janeiro
Contract size   Index × Cr$5
Minimum price move (value)   1.0 (Cr$5)
Trading months   February, April, June, August, October,
   December
Trading hours   0930–1315

Brazil

Contract   IBOVESPA Stock Index Option
Exchange   Bolsa Brasileira de Futuros
Contract size   Index × Cr$5.0
Minimum price move (value)   0.01
Trading months   February, April, June, August, October, December
Trading hours   0930–1315
Expiry   Friday before futures delivery
Style   Calls American, puts European

Brazil

Contract   IBOVESPA Stock Index Future
Exchange   Bolsa Mercantil de Futuros, São Paulo
Contract size   Index × Czs$0.5
Minimum price move (value)   5.0 (Czs$2.5)
Settlement   Business day following last trading day
Trading months   February, April, June, August, October, December
Trading hours   0930–1315
Expiry   The Wednesday nearest to the 15th day of the contract month

Canada

Contract   Toronto 35 Index Future
Exchange   Toronto Future Exchange
Contract size   Index × C$500
Minimum price move (value)   0.02 (C$10)
Settlement   Second business day after last trade day
Trading months   Nearest three months
Trading hours   0915-1615
Expiry   Thursday before third Friday of contract month
Position limits   1000 contracts speculative; 2200 contracts hedge position
Daily price limits   13.5 points

Canada

Contract   Toronto 35 Index Option
Exchange   Toronto Futures Exchange
Contract size   Index × C$100
Minimum price move   0.02
Settlement   On second business day after last trade day
Trading months   Nearest three months plus some longer term options
Trading hours   0930–1615
Expiry   Day after last trade day
Last trading day   Thursday before third Friday of contract month
Style   European

Canada

Contract   Toronto Stock Exchange 300 Composite Stock Index Future
Exchange   Toronto Futures Exchange
Contract size   Index × C$10
Minimum price move (value)   1.0 (C$10)
Settlement   At end of each day
Trading   Daily; no overnight positions
Trading hours   0920–1610
Expiry   Daily
Position limits   2000 contracts

Denmark

Contract   KFX 25 Stock Index Future
Exchange   FUTOP Copenhagen
Contract size   Index × DKK1000
Minimum price move (value)   0.05 (DKK50)
Settlement   On expiry day
Trading months   March, June, September, December
Trading hours   0900–1530
Expiry   First day of contract month
Last trading day   Day before expiry

Denmark

Contract   KFX 25 Stock Index Option
Exchange   FUTOP Copenhagen
Contract size   Index × DKK1000
Minimum price move (value)   0.05 (DKK50)
Settlement   On expiry
Trading months   March, June, September, December
Trading hours   0900–1530
Expiry   First trading day of contract month
Last trading day   Day preceding expiry day
Style   European

Finland

Contract   FOX 25 Stock Index Future
Exchange   Finnish Options Market
Contract size   Index × FIM100
Minimum price move (value)   FIM0.5 (FIM50)
Settlement   Five days after expiry
Trading months   Nearest two months from the February, April, June, August, October, December cycle
Trading hours   1000–1600
Expiry   Fourth Friday of expiry month
Last trading day   Day before expiry

Finland

Contract   FOX 25 Stock Index Option
Exchange   Finnish Options Exchange
Contract size   Index × FIM100
Minimum price move (value)   0.05 (FIM5)
Settlement   Three days after expiry
Trading months   February, April, June, August, October, December
Trading hours   1000–1630
Expiry   Third Friday of contract month
Last trading day   Thursday before expiry
Style   European

France

Contract   CAC-40 Index Future
Exchange   Matif
Contract size   Index × FF200
Minimum price move (value)   0.1 (FF25)
Settlement   Day after trade day
Trading months   First three months plus one quarterly cycle
   month (March, June, September, December)
Trading hours   1000–1700
Expiry   Last business day in contract month

France

Contract   CAC-40 Index Option
Exchange   MONEP Paris
Contract size   Index × FF200
Minimum price move (value)   0.01 (FF2)
Settlement   On expiry
Trading months   Nearest three months plus March, June,
   September, December cycle
Trading hours   1030–1700
Expiry   Last business day of trading month
Style   American

Germany

Contract   DAX Stock Index Future
Exchange   DTB
Contract size   Index × DM100
Minimum price move (value)   0.5 (DM50)
Settlement   On business day following last trade day
Trading months   March, June, September, December
Trading hours   1030–1345
Expiry   Third Friday of contract month
Last trading day   Day before expiry

Germany

Contract   DAX Stock Index Option
Exchange   DTB

Contract size   Index × DM10
Minimum price move (value)   0.1 (DM1)
Settlement   Business day following expiry
Trading months   Nearest three months plus next two of the
   March, June, September, December cycle
Trading hours   0930–1600
Last trading day   Third Friday of contract month
Style   European

Hong Kong

Contract   Hang Seng Index Future
Exchange   Hong Kong Futures Exchange
Contract size   Index × HK$50
Minimum price move (value)   1.0 (HK$50)
Settlement   On business day following last trade day
Trading months   Nearest two months plus next two months
   from March, June, September, December
Trading hours   1000–1230, 1430–1530
Expiry   Second last business day of contract month
Daily price limits   300 points per session

Ireland

Contract   ISEQ Index Future
Exchange   IFOX Dublin
Contract size   Index × Ir£10
Minimum price move (value)   0.01 (Ir£1)
Settlement   On expiry day
Trading months   March, June, September, December
Trading hours   0830–1615
Expiry   Business day prior to third Thursday of contract month
Daily price limits   50 points

Japan

Contract   25 Stock Index Option
Exchange   Nagoya Stock Exchange
Contract size   Index × ¥10000
Minimum price move (value)   1.0 (¥10000)

Settlement   On expiry
Trading months   Nearest four months
Trading hours   0900–1100, 1300–1510
Expiry   Business day preceding second Friday of contract month
Last trading day   Thursday before expiry Friday
Style   European

Japan

Contract   Nikkei 225 Index Future
Exchange   Osaka Stock Exchange
Contract size   Index × ¥1000
Minimum price move (value)   10.0 (¥10000)
Settlement   Cash
Trading months   March, June, September, December
Trading hours   0900–1100, 1300–1510
Expiry   Special quotation on opening level of index constituents on day after last trade day
Last trading day   Thursday before second Friday of month

Japan

Contract   Nikkei 225 Index Option
Exchange   Osaka Stock Exchange
Contract size   Index × ¥1000
Minimum price move (value)   10.0 (¥10000)
Settlement   On expiry
Trading months   Nearest four months
Trading hours   0900–1100, 1300–1510
Expiry   As last trading day, but allowance made so that futures do not expire at same time
Last trading day   Thursday before second Friday of contract month
Style   Weekly exercise (Thursdays)

Japan

Contract   TOPIX Future
Exchange   Tokyo Stock Exchange
Contract size   Index × ¥10000

Minimum price move (value) 1.0 (¥10000)
Settlement Cash
Trading months March, June, September, December
Trading hours 0900–1100, 1300–1510
Expiry Special quotation on opening level of index constituents on day after last trade day
Last trading day Thursday before second Friday of month
Daily price limits 60 points

Japan

Contract TOPIX Option
Exchange Tokyo Stock Exchange
Contract size Index × ¥10000
Minimum price move (value) 0.5 (¥5000)
Settlement On expiry
Trading months Nearest four months
Trading hours 0900–1100, 1300–1510
Expiry As last trading day, but allowance made so that futures do not expire at same time
Last trading day Thursday before second Friday of contract month
Daily price limits 60 points
Style American

Japan

Contract OSF 50 Stock Index Future
Exchange Osaka Securities Exchange
Contract size Total of the shares representing one unit of trade, normally 1000 shares in each of the 50 underlying stocks
Minimum price move (value) ¥0.5 per unit (minimum of ¥25000 per contract)
Settlement Physical delivery of the stocks on expiry
Trading months March, June, September, December
Trading hours 0900–1115, 0100–0315
Delivery The fifteenth day of the contract month, or the next business day after this if the fifteenth is not a business day
Last trading day The sixth business day prior to delivery

Netherlands

Contract   EOE Dutch Stock Index Future
Exchange   EOE Amsterdam
Contract size   Index × FL200
Minimum price move (value)   0.1 (FL20)
Settlement   Cash
Trading months   Nearest three months plus January, April, July, October
Trading hours   1015–1630
Expiry   Third Friday of contract month
Position limits   8000 contracts

Netherlands

Contract   EOE Dutch Stock Index Option
Exchange   EOE Amsterdam
Contract size   Index × FL100
Minimum price move (value)   0.1 (FL10)
Settlement   Business day after expiry
Trading months   Nearest three months then 6, 9 and 12 months in January, April, July, October cycle
Trading hours   1030–1630
Expiry   Saturday following third Friday of contract month
Last trading day   Third Friday of contract month
Position limits   8000 contracts
Style   European

Netherlands

Contract   Dutch Top5 Index Future
Exchange   EOE Amsterdam
Contract size   Index × FL200
Minimum price move (value)   0.1 (FL20)
Settlement   Cash
Trading months   Nearest three months plus January, April, July, October
Trading hours   1005–1630
Expiry   Third Friday of contract month
Position limits   4000 contracts

Netherlands

Contract   Dutch Top5 Index Options
Exchange   EOE Amsterdam
Contract size   Index × FL100
Minimum price move (value)   0.1 (FL10)
Settlement   Business day after expiry
Trading months   Nearest three months then 6, 9 and 12 months in January, April, July, October cycle
Trading hours   1030–1630
Expiry   Saturday following third Friday of contract month
Last trading day   Third Friday of contract monthly
Position limits   4000 contracts
Style   European

Netherlands

Contract   Major Market Index Option
Exchange   EOE Amsterdam (and AMEX)
Contract size   Index × US$100
Minimum price move (value)   US$⅛
Settlement   On expiry
Trading months   Nearest three months
Trading hours   1200–1630
Expiry   Saturday following third Friday of expiry month
Last trading day   Third Friday of contract month
Position limits   10000 contracts
Style   European

New Zealand

Contract   Barclays Share Price Index Future
Exchange   New Zealand Futures and Options Exchange
Contract size   Index × NZ$20
Minimum price move (value)   1.0 (NZ$20)
Settlement   Day after last trade day
Trading months   Nearest three months plus March, June, September, December
Trading hours   0900–1650
Expiry   Second to last business day of settlement month

New Zealand

Contract   Barclays Share Price Index Option
Exchange   New Zealand Futures and Options Exchange
Contract size   Index × NZ$20
Minimum price move (value)   1.0 (NZ$20)
Settlement   On expiry
Trading months   March, June, September, December
Trading hours   0900–1650
Expiry   Day preceding last business day of contract month
Style   American

Norway

Contract   OBX Index Option
Exchange   Oslo Stock Exchange
Contract size   Index × NKr100
Minimum price move (value)   0.01 (NKr1.0)
Settlement   Third business day after trading
Trading months   All calendar months
Trading hours   1000–1500
Expiry   Second Friday of expiry month
Last trading day   Day preceding expiry
Style   European

Singapore

Contract   Nikkei Stock Average Future
Exchange   SIMEX
Contract size   Index × ¥500
Minimum price move (value)   5.0 (¥2500)
Settlement   On last trade day
Trading months   March, June, September, December
Trading hours   0800–1415
Expiry   Third Wednesday of contract month
Position limits   1000 contracts

South Africa

Contract   JSE Actuaries All Industrial Index Future
Exchange   SAFEX

Contract size   Index × R10
Minimum price move (value)   1.0 (R10)
Settlement   Cash
Trading months   March, June, September, December
Trading hours   24-hour screen trading; mark to market price at 1630
Expiry   15th day of contract month

Spain

Contract   MEFF 30 Stock Index Future
Exchange   Mercado de Futuros Financieros SA Barcelona
Contract size   Index × PTAS500
Minimum price move (value)   1.0 (PTAS500)
Settlement   On business day following last trade day
Trading months   Nearest three months plus last month of following quarter
Trading hours   1030–1730
Expiry   Fourth Wednesday of contract month
Last trading day   Two days before expiry

Sweden

Contract   OMX 30 Index Future
Exchange   OM Stockholm
Contract size   Index × SEK100
Minimum price move (value)   0.01 (SEK1)
Settlement   Physical or cash on fifth day after expiry
Trading months   Nearest, second and fourth month
Trading hours   1000–1600
Expiry   Fourth Friday in contract month
Last trading day   Day before expiry day

Sweden

Contract   OMX 30 Index Option
Exchange   OM Stockholm
Contract size   Index × Skr100
Minimum price move (value)   0.01 (Skr1.0)
Settlement   Fifth business day after trading

Trading months   All calendar months
Trading hours   1000–1600
Expiry   Fourth Friday of expiry month
Last trading day   Day preceding expiry
Style   European

Switzerland

Contract   Swiss Market Index Future
Exchange   SOFFEX Zurich
Contract size   Index × SF50
Minimum price move (value)   0.1 (SF5)
Settlement   Day after last trade day
Trading months   Nearest three months plus January, April, July, October
Trading hours   1000–1300, 1400–1600
Expiry   Third Friday of contract month (1130)

Switzerland

Contract   Swiss Market Index Option
Exchange   SOFFEX, Zurich
Contract size   Index × SF5
Minimum price move (value)   0.1 (SF0.5)
Settlement   On expiry
Trading months   Nearest three months plus January, April, July, October cycle
Trading hours   1000–1300, 1400–1615
Expiry   Saturday after third Friday of contract month
Last trading day   Third Friday of contract month
Style   European

UK

Contract   FT-SE 100 Index Future
Exchange   LIFFE
Contract size   Index × £25
Minimum price move (value)   0.5 (£12.50)
Settlement   Day after last trade day
Trading months   March, June, September, December

Trading hours   0835–1600 (1632–1730 electronic)
Expiry   Last business day in contract month (1130)

UK

Contract   FT-SE 100 Index Option
Exchange   LTOM
Contract size   Index × £10
Minimum price move (value)   0.5 (£5)
Settlement   On expiry
Trading months   Nearest four months plus June and December
Trading hours   0835–1610
Expiry   Last business day of expiry month
Style   American

UK

Contract   FT-SE 100 Index Option
Exchange   LTOM
Contract size   Index × £10
Minimum price move (value)   0.5 (£5)
Settlement   On expiry
Trading months   Nearest two months then March, June, September, December cycle
Trading hours   0835–1610
Expiry   Last business day of contract month
Style   European

UK

Contract   FT-SE Eurotrack 100 Index Future
Exchange   LIFFE
Contract size   Index × DM100
Minimum price move (value)   0.5 (DM50)
Settlement   First business day after last trading day
Trading months   March, June, September, December
Trading hours   0915–1545
Expiry   Third Friday in contract month (1120)

UK

Contract   FT-SE Eurotrack 100 Index Option
Exchange   LTOM
Contract size   Index × DM50
Minimum price move (value)   0.5 (DM25)
Settlement   On expiry
Trading months   Nearest three months plus March, June,
   September, December cycle
Trading hours   0915–1545
Expiry   Last trading day
Last trading day   Third Friday of contract month
Style   European

UK

Contract   German Equity Market Index
Exchange   OM London
Contract size   Index × DM10
Settlement   Five German business days after expiry
Trading months   Nearest three months plus six months
   introduced every three months
Trading hours   0830–1500
Expiry   Third Friday of contract month
Last trading day   Day preceding expiry

UK

Contract   German Equity Market Option
Exchange   OM London
Contract size   Index × DM10
Settlement   German business days after expiry
Trading months   Nearest three months plus six months;
   introduced every three months
Trading hours   0830–1500
Expiry   Third Friday of contract month
Last trading day   Business day preceding expiry
Style   European

UK

Contract   OMX 30 Swedish Index Future
Exchange   OM London
Contract size   Index × SEK100
Minimum price move (value)   0.01 (SEK1)
Settlement   Physical or cash on fifth day after expiry
Trading months   Nearest, second and fourth month
Trading hours   0900–1500
Expiry   Fourth Friday in contract month
Last trading day   Day before expiry day

UK

Contract   OMX Swedish Index Option
Exchange   OM London
Contract size   Index × Skr100
Minimum price move (value)   0.01 (Skr1.0)
Settlement   Fifth day after expiry
Trading months   All calendar months
Trading hours   0900–1500
Expiry   Fourth Friday of contract month
Last trading day   Day preceding expiry day
Style   European

USA

Contract   Computer Technology Stock Index Option
Exchange   American Stock Exchange
Contract size   Index × US$100
Minimum price move (value) $\frac{1}{16}$ point (US$6.25)
Settlement   On expiry
Trading months   Nearest three months plus next two of January, April, July, October cycle
Trading hours   0930–1610
Expiry   Business day following last trading day
Last trading day   Third Friday of contract month
Position limits   8000 contracts
Style   American

USA

Contract   Institutional Index Option
Exchange   American Stock Exchange
Contract size   Index × US$100
Minimum price move (value) $1/16\text{th}$–$1/8\text{th}$ points (US$6.25–12.5)
Settlement   Day after trading
Trading months   Nearest three months then March, June, September, December cycle
Trading hours   0930–1615
Expiry   Saturday following third Friday of contract month
Last trading day   Business day preceding expiry day
Style   European

USA

Contract   International Market Index Future
Exchange   NY Coffee, Sugar and Cocoa Exchange
Contract size   Index × US$250
Minimum price move (value)   0.05 (US$12.50)
Settlement   Business day after last trade day
Trading months   Nearest three months plus March, June, September, December
Trading hours   0930–1615
Expiry   Business day preceding third Friday in contract month
Position limits   5000 contracts

USA

Contract   International Market Index Option
Exchange   American Stock Exchange
Contract size   Index × US$100
Minimum price move (value) $1/16$–$1/8$ points (US$6.25–12.5)
Settlement   Day after trading
Trading months   Nearest three months plus March, June, September, December cycle
Trading hours   0930–1615
Expiry   Saturday following third Friday of contract month

Last trading day   Two business days before expiry
Style   European

USA

Contract   Major Market Index Future
Exchange   Chicago Board of Trade
Contract size   Index × US$250
Minimum price move (value)   0.05 (US$12.50)
Settlement   Cash
Trading months   Every month
Trading hours   0815–1515
Expiry   Third Friday of contract month
Position limits   8000 contracts

USA

Contract   Major Market Index Option
Exchange   American Stock Exchange (and EOE)
Contract size   Index × US$100
Minimum price move (value) $\frac{1}{16}$–$\frac{1}{8}$ points (US$6.25–12.5)
Settlement   Day after trading
Trading months   Nearest three months
Trading hours   0930–1615
Expiry   Saturday following third Friday of contract month
Last trading day   Day preceding expiry day
Position limits   17000 contracts
Style   European

USA

Contract   NYSE Composite Index Future
Exchange   New York Futures Exchange
Contract size   Index × US$500
Minimum price move (value)   0.05 (US$25)
Settlement   Cash
Trading months   March, June, September, December
Trading hours   0930–1615
Expiry   Thursday before third Friday of contract month
Position limits   10000 contracts

USA

Contract   NYSE Composite Index Option (or Future)
Exchange   NY Futures Exchange
Contract size   Index × US$500
Minimum price move (value)   0.05 (US$25)
Settlement   On expiry
Trading months   Nearest three months plus March, June, September, December cycle
Trading hours   0930–1615
Expiry   Last trading day (or day after for quarterly cycles)
Last trading day   Third Friday of contract month (or day before for quarterly cycles)
Position limits   10000 contracts
Style   American

USA

Contract   NYSE Composite Index Option
Exchange   NY Stock Exchange
Contract size   Index × US$100
Minimum price move (value) $\frac{1}{16}$ point (US$6.25)
Settlement   On expiry
Trading months   Nearest three months
Trading hours   0930–1615
Expiry   Saturday after last trading day
Last trading day   Third Friday of contract month
Style   American

USA

Contract   Oil Stock Index Option
Exchange   American Stock Exchange
Contract size   Index × US$100
Minimum price move (value) $\frac{1}{16}$ point (US$6.25)
Settlement   On expiry
Trading months   Nearest three months plus January, April, July, October cycle
Trading hours   0930–1610
Expiry   Business day following last trading day

Last trading day   Third Friday of contract month
Position limits   8000 contracts
Style   American

USA

Contract   S & P 500 Index Future
Exchange   CME
Contract size   Index × US$500
Minimum price move (value)   0.05 (US$25)
Settlement   Cash on third Friday of contract month
Trading months   March, June, September, December
Trading hours   0830–1515
Expiry   Business day preceding the third Friday of contract month
Position limits   5000 contracts

USA

Contract   S & P 500 Index Option
Exchange   CME
Contract size   Index × US$500
Minimum price move (value)   0.05 (US$25)
Settlement   On expiry
Trading months   Nearest three months plus March, June, September, December cycle
Trading hours   0830–1515
Expiry   Third Friday of month
Last trading day   Business day prior to expiry
Position limits   5000 futures equivalent
Style   American

USA

Contract   S & P 500 Index Option
Exchange   CBOE
Contract size   Index × US$100
Minimum price move (value)   1.0 (US$100)
Settlement   Business day after expiry
Trading months   Nearest two months plus March, June,

September, December cycle; longer periods can also be
obtained
Trading hours   0830–1515
Expiry   Business day after last trading day
Last trading day   Third Friday of contract month
Style   European

USA

Contract   S & P 500 Index Option
Exchange   CBOE
Contract size   Index × US$100
Minimum price move (value) $\frac{1}{16}$–$\frac{1}{8}$ points
  (US$6.25–12.50)
Settlement   Business day after expiry
Trading months   Nearest three months plus March, June,
  September, December cycle
Trading hours   0830–1515
Expiry   Business day after last trading day
Last trading day   Third Friday of contract month
Style   American

USA

Contract   Value Line Index Future
Exchange   Kansas City BOT
Contract size   Index × US$100
Minimum price move (value)   0.05 (US$5)
Settlement   Cash on expiry
Trading months   Nearest six months in March, June,
  September, December cycle
Trading hours   0830–1515
Expiry   Third Friday of contract month
Position limits   5000 contracts

USA

Contract   Value Line Composite Index Option
Exchange   Philadelphia Stock Exchange
Contract size   Index × US$100

Minimum price move (value) $\frac{1}{16\text{th}} - \frac{1}{8\text{th}}$ points
(US\$ 6.25–12.5)
Settlement   On expiry
Trading months   Nearest two months plus March, June,
September, December cycle
Trading hours   0930–1615
Expiry   Saturday following last trading day
Last trading day   Third Friday in contract month
Style   European

USA

Contract   Mini Value Line Index Future
Exchange   Kansas City BOT
Contract size   Index × US\$100
Minimum price move (value)   0.05 (US\$5)
Settlement   Cash on expiry
Trading months   Nearest six months in March, June,
September, December cycle
Trading hours   0830–1515
Expiry   Third Friday of contract month
Position limits   5000 contracts

USA

Contract   TOPIX Future
Exchange   CBOT
Contract size   Index × ¥5000
Minimum price move (value)   0.5 (¥2500)
Settlement   Cash ¥en on expiry
Trading months   March, June, September, December
Trading hours   0815–1515, 1800–2015
Expiry   Business day preceding the second Friday of the
contract month
Position limits   8000 contracts
Daily price limits   70 index points

USA

Contract   TOPIX Option
Exchange   CBOT

Contract size   Index × ¥5000
Minimum price move (value)   0.5 (¥2500)
Settlement   One futures contract
Trading months   March, June, September, December
Trading hours   0815–1515
Expiry   Second Friday of contract month
Last trading day   Business day preceding expiry
Position limits   8000 contracts
Daily price limits   70 index points
Style   American

USA

Contract   Nikkei 225 Index Future
Exchange   CME
Contract size   Index × US$5
Minimum price move (value)   5.0 (US$25)
Settlement   Cash US$ on expiry
Trading months   March, June, September, December
Trading hours   0800–1515
Expiry   Business day preceding the second Friday of the
  contract month
Position limits   5000 contracts

USA

Contract   Japan (210 Stock) Index Option
Exchange   American Stock Exchange
Contract size   Index × US$100
Minimum price move (value) $\frac{1}{16}$–$\frac{1}{8}$ points (US$6.25–12.50)
Settlement   On expiry
Trading months   Nearest three months plus longer term expiry
  months
Trading hours   0930–1615
Expiry   Saturday after last trading day
Last trading day   Third Friday of contract month
Style   European

Glossary of terms

Abandonment Allowing an option or warrant to expire unexercised.

American style An option that may be exercised at any time before expiry.

Arbitrage The purchase of a commodity or financial instrument in one market and the simultaneous sale of an equivalent instrument in a different market in order to benefit from pricing discrepancies.

Assignment Formal notification that an option or warrant writer must buy or sell the underlying security at the exercise price.

At-the-money An option or warrant where the exercise price is at the same level as the current price of the underlying security.

Backwardation When the price of nearby futures is at a premium to more distant futures.

Basis The difference between the futures contract and its underlying cash instrument.

Bear One who expects the market to decline.

Beta Statistical measure of the sensitivity of the movement of an equity price to the movement of the whole market.

Bull One who expects the market to rise.

Call option A contract that gives the buyer the right, but not the obligation, to buy the underlying index at a specified price within a predetermined period of time.

Cash market Market with immediate delivery.

Cash price Price for the cash market.

Class Option types, i.e. calls or puts.

Clearing house The organization that guarantees performance and oversees settlement of exchange traded contracts.

Closing trade The transaction required to close an open position and so terminate liability.

Contango When nearby prices stand at a discount to forward prices.

Contract Standard unit of trading for futures or options.

Contract month Specific month to which a futures or options contract relates.

Convergence Narrowing of the futures/cash differential as the contract progresses towards expiry.

Cost of carry Equivalent to fair-value. The cost of maintaining a cash position.

Crude basis The difference between the index and the traded level of its futures contract.

Delta Change of option premium for incremental change in the underlying index.

EDSP Exchange Delivery Settlement Price—the price at which options or futures are settled, on expiry.

European style An option that can only be exercised on the expiry date.

Exercise The formal notification that the holder of an option wishes to exercise the right to buy or sell the underlying index at the exercise price.

Exercise price The price at which the holder of an option or warrant can buy or sell the underlying index.

Expiry date The last day on which an option or warrant can be exercised.

Fair-value The theoretical level at which a contract should trade relative to its underlying index.

Floor broker A broker who has a presence on the exchange and undertakes order execution in exchange for a fee.

Future A legally binding agreement to make or take delivery of a specified quantity and quality of a specified instrument at a fixed date in the future, at a price agreed at the time of dealing.

Gamma The rate of change of delta for an incremental change in the underlying index.

Gearing The increased ratio of profits or losses generated when using a small investment to obtain larger exposure.

Hedging Reduction of risk by opening an opposite position through futures options or warrants to that already held in the underlying market.

Initial margin A returnable deposit required by the clearing house as protection against default from contracts entered into by futures traders or option writers.

In-the-money A call (or put) where the exercise price is below (or above) the current market level.

Intrinsic value The degree to which a call or put is in-the-money.

Last trading day Final day for trading a contract in its expiry month.

Mark to market Daily valuation of open futures positions in order to reflect profits or losses. Based on settlement prices.

Open interest The net amount of outstanding positions in a particular futures or options contract.

Open outcry The method of trading where bids and offers are made audibly to other traders on an exchange floor.

Opening trade A transaction that creates a new position.

Out-of-the-money An option or warrant in which the exercise price is above the underlying index for a call, below for a put.

Parity Futures contracts when trading at the same level as the cash index.

Pit Designated area within an exchange where a particular contract is traded.

Position limit A limit imposed by some exchanges on the number of contracts that any one party may hold.

Premium The option price.

Put option A contract that gives the buyer the right, but not the obligation, to sell the underlying index at a specified price within a predetermined period of time.

Rho The effect on an options value of a 1 per cent rise in interest rates.

Roll-over The transfer of a near futures or options position to a further contract, involving the closing of the near position and simultaneous opening of the further new position.

Round trip The completed contract, opening and closing. Dealing costs are normally quoted on a round trip basis.

Series Options of the same class with the same exercise and expiry date.

Settlement price Price used for daily revaluation of open positions.

Spot Alternative term for cash or prompt.

Spreads Options (and futures) transactions involving two or more series of the underlying index.

Spread margin A concessionary reduced margin allowed for the limited risk trades undertaken by spread traders in futures contracts, (i.e. long near month, short forward)

Strike price Alternative term for exercise price.

Systematic risk Risk inherent in the market as a whole, i.e. interest rates, political factors. Measured by beta.

Tail Adjustment to a futures position to allow for the effect of variation margin on the efficiency of a hedge or arbitrage position.

Theta Decline in option premium with time.

Tick The smallest unit by which the price of a futures or options contract can move.

Time value The amount by which an option premium exceeds its intrinsic value, and reflects the period remaining before expiry.

Unsystematic risk Risk of a stock associated with factors unique to the stock, i.e. company profitability, labour relations, new developments.

Variation margin Payment made in order to restore or maintain initial margin on adverse positions.

Volatility Statistical measurement of share price movement over a standard time period.

Warrant Similar to an option but with a much longer time frame, and normally traded outside formal exchanges.

Writer The person who executes the opening sale of a warrant or option.

Bibliography

Dickson, M. *Guide to Financial Times Statistics.* Financial Times Business Information 1989

Frost, A. J. and R. Prechter. *Elliott Wave Principle.* McGraw-Hill 1991

FT-SE Share Indices. London Stock Exchange 1991

Gann, W. D. *How to Make Profits in Commodities.* W. D. Gann Holdings Inc. 1951

Luskin, D. L. *Portfolio Insurance. A Guide to Dynamic Hedging.* J. Wiley & Son 1988

McMillan, L. G. *Options as a Strategic Investment.* New York Institute of Finance 1986

Robertson, M. *Directory of World Futures and Options.* Woodhead-Faulkner 1991

Teweles, R. J., C. V. Harlow and H. L. Stone. *The Commodity Futures Game.* McGraw-Hill 1977

Vince, R. *Portfolio Management Formulas, Mathematical Trading Methods for Futures Options and Stock Markets.* J. Wiley & Son 1991

Index